Reader to Reader

Building Independence Through Peer Partnerships

Mary Lee Prescott-Griffin

Heinemann
Portsmouth, NH

Heinemann

A division of Reed Elsevier Inc.
361 Hanover Street
Portsmouth, NH 03801–3912
www.heinemann.com

Offices and agents throughout the world

Library of Congress Cataloging-in-Publication Data
Prescott-Griffin, Mary Lee.
   Reader to reader : building independence through peer partnerships /
Mary Lee Prescott-Griffin.
     p. cm.
   Includes bibliographical references and index.
   ISBN 0-325-00609-1 (alk. paper)
   1. Reading (Primary).   2. Peer-group tutoring of students.
3. Group reading.   I. Title.
LB1525.P76 2005
372.4—dc22   2004027989

Editor: Kate Montgomery
Production editor: Sonja S. Chapman
Cover design: Jenny Jensen Greenleaf
Compositor: Technologies 'N Typography
Manufacturing: Louise Richardson

Printed in the United States of America on acid-free paper
09   08   07   06   05   RRD   1   2   3   4   5

To my parents, Louise and Winward Prescott,
whose love and quiet pride have made all the difference.

Contents

Acknowledgments

So many people have helped and supported me in the writing of this book. I am especially indebted to my first-grade students, their parents, and the administration of Friends Academy for making the initial study of peer partnerships possible. Through their actions and words, my students forever changed my ideas and beliefs about what it means to be literate. Grateful acknowledgement also goes to the faculties of Rhode Island College and the University of Rhode Island for their encouragement in the earliest stages of my research. Most especially, I want to thank Joan Glazer, adviser and friend, for her unfailing support, sage advice, and wonderful sense of humor—the latter interjected at the most opportune moments.

My gratitude and abiding respect go to first-grade teachers Sharon Roberts, Kristin Vito, Christine Wiltshire, Sarah Rich, Joy Richardson, Anne Santoro, Jo-Ann Gettings, Cheryl Feeney, Gia Renaud, and Jenny Baumeister for inviting me into their classrooms and for so generously sharing their expertise. As they strive to make peer partnerships work in their classrooms with their students, they each implement the model somewhat differently. This diversity continues to make the study of peer partner reading so fascinating and compelling.

As a seasoned educator, one of the true delights of classroom research is discovering what children can teach me about reading and literacy instruction. In taking my work beyond my own classroom, I have had the privilege and pleasure of observing hundreds of children at work in partnership. My warm and heartfelt thanks is therefore extended to the students and administrators of the

L. G. Nourse School, in Norton, Massachusetts; the Fairlawn Early Learning Center, in Lincoln, Rhode Island; the Paul Cuffee Charter School, in Providence, Rhode Island; the Hugh Cole School, in Warren, Rhode Island; the Spencer Borden School, in Fall River, Massachusetts; and the Mills Pond School, in Smithtown, New York, for sharing so much with me over the years. Always, it is the students who bring alive and give voice to my nascent theories about reading in social context.

Many people have assisted me with my work, arranging research placements and offering much needed encouragement and support. I am especially grateful to my student research assistant, Heather Brennan, for her work during the L. G. Nourse study. Also, for their help "along the way," I thank Nancy Fletcher, Lorraine Conway, Beverly Paesano, Melinda Foley-Marsello, Emily Goff, Claudia Daggett, David Bourns, Suzie Shaw, Josie Woollam, Gerry Smith, Arlene Wild, and Sam Bertolino.

To Kate Montgomery, editor extraordinaire, I send many kudos. Every step of the way, her enthusiasm and excitement about this project has made such an enormous difference, especially as I tore up and revised the manuscript again and again. I am also grateful to Alan Huisman for his skillful copyediting, which provided a much-needed road map for the revision journey and to Sonja Chapman and all at Heinemann for guiding the book through production.

Finally, I want to thank my family and friends for their support, encouragement, and love. This book has come to life during tumultuous times, and I could never have stayed the course without so many people at my side. A mother's thanks to my sons, Ransom and Winward, for always making me laugh and for stirring the seeds of this study years ago as they began their messy, exhilarating, and deeply personal journeys to literacy. I am also grateful to my strong, wise daughter-in-law, Stephanie, for her support and love. And last, but not least, to my incredible sisters, Betty, Pamela, and Louise Prescott: there really are no words. If I have any sense, wisdom, or strength, it comes from my association with you and our dear parents.

Introduction

I think the biggest misconception about peer partnerships is that you can't do them with little kids. Everyone says they can't read, yet they can!

—Sharon Roberts, first-grade teacher

This book explores peer partnerships, a reading strategy in which beginning readers of approximately equal expertise construct text together side by side. It is also about how teachers help young readers build text and literate understanding together. First graders have definite thoughts and opinions about the constructive, collaborative nature of reading partnerships as well as the scaffolds and companionship they share during the sometimes challenging work of reading "independently." So, finally, the book is about teachers listening to what children say and do and how they demonstrate the strategies and instructional practices that best serve their needs.

Although many teacher-to-teacher suggestions are included here, you will also hear many suggestions from children. The learning communities described are ones in which all participants—teachers *and* students—have a say in how teaching and learning will happen. In these classrooms, teachers instruct, model, and demonstrate, then step back and trust children to work constructively together, building theories and knowledge about reading as they practice and develop literacy skills and strategies.

The book is based on my work in eleven classrooms in seven different schools. Although my research is always child-centered, focused on what children's words and actions tell us about their learning needs, always it is the teachers' voices that provide the background and context for what their students are saying and doing. Their literacy programs are described in Appendix N. Although these programs share some components, they often differ considerably. This is intentional. I hope you will find some common ground between your program and at least one of those described, so that you can better envision how peer partnerships might fit into your classroom.

Effective, reflective teaching is central to this book. Some of the teachers whose work is represented here have been in the classroom only a few years, and others have five, ten, or more years of experience. But they have a number of important things in common:

- They are committed to professionalism and lifelong learning in order to best serve the diverse learning needs of their students.

- They do not deliver a one-size-fits-all reading curriculum by reading scripts created outside their classroom. They teach in active, thoughtful ways based on their knowledge of reading pedagogy and their students.

- They are committed to listening to students, assessing not only their academic needs but their emotional and social needs as well.

- They teach in schools with strong ongoing professional development programs.

- They teach in schools in which teachers, students, and administrators continually examine curriculum and methods for ways to improve teaching and learning.

- They teach in schools whose leaders foster collegiality and the sharing of ideas and teaching strategies.

- They use school/district/state literacy frameworks, standards, and structures to plan lessons and reading programs; school and district administrators support them in selecting the most appropriate methods and materials to meet the needs of their students.

- They respond to students in genuine, thoughtful, informed ways.

Throughout the book, in addition to offering teaching tools and techniques, I highlight and celebrate the incredible teaching that goes on every day in schools in which teachers' professionalism is respected and students' thoughts about effective strategies for helping one another are valued and celebrated. Peer partnerships are flexible and adapt to many programs and curriculums. My first graders begin working in peer partnerships on the first day of school because I find the strategy to be very supportive of early reading development. Other teachers offer partner reading as a choice during reading workshop, sustained silent reading, or independent reading. Teachers may also choose to begin partnerships midyear, or pair readers who are unable to be productive independently.

Peer partnerships are not new, nor are they particularly revolutionary. Primary-grade teachers have been using them for years to give children extra practice. Practice does, indeed, build young readers' fluency and helps them enjoy reading more; however, successful partnerships depend on readers' understanding of collaboration. The key to learning, according to Vygotsky (1978), does not lie in the child's innate ability but in the social support received from adults or peers. Primary-grade peer partners support each other in many ways, sharing expertise as they structure and define what it means to read together. Vygotsky defined the zone of proximal development as "the distance between the actual developmental level as determined by independent problem solving and the level of potential development as determined through problem solving under adult guidance or in collaboration with more capable peers" (p. 86). My observations suggest that the role of capable peer shifts many times when children read together.

Although research supports the value of peer partnerships, it is not enough to pair children and send them on their way. As teachers, we must recognize our students' cognitive, social, and emotional needs and so be able to pair readers who will grow into successful collaborators. We must also observe peer partnerships in action and offer explicit teaching and modeling to support collaboration. Lessons focused on partner reading give children a forum in which to share the effective collaboration strategies they use. These sessions also provide opportunities for powerful teacher and student modeling.

Classrooms in which teachers and students have spent time building community and trust tend to incorporate peer reading partnerships more smoothly. Classrooms in which teachers model and discuss their own reading, thus letting their students in on their literate thinking processes, provide fertile ground for these social relationships.

The chapters that follow will help you plan and implement peer partnerships throughout the school year. You'll find suggestions for how to create environments that support reader collaborations and how to encourage and celebrate child-centered strategies. Vignettes of children supporting and scaffolding each other's literacy learning let you see peer partnerships in action. You'll also find ideas about how to get children to take turns effectively and how the roles partners assume enhance or hinder collaboration. Variations like buddy circles and buddy reading centers are included, as these structures may best suit certain students and programs. Finally, many classrooms include students with special needs or students who are already fluent readers; you'll also find ideas for adapting peer partnerships to suit these primary-grade readers.

Remember, there is no one "right way" to use peer partnerships. As you read the teacher stories and techniques outlined here, pick and choose the models that serve your students and programs at a particular time.

Getting Started

1

Clattering footsteps herald the start of an October school day. My first graders make their way down the stairs, stopping first at cubbies to store backpacks and lunches. Then, papers and other materials in hand, they enter the room, chatting with friends and waving to students in the adjoining first-grade classroom. Every child shakes my hand, then reads the morning message and the task outlined at the bottom (usually a math question, something short to read, or a journal entry). Standing side by side, children help each other read the message before moving away to get organized and complete the task. Finally, they find their partner and settle down to read.

Kitty and Emma sit side by side at a table, a stack of decodable readers between them. (Although I neither promote nor discourage choosing decodable texts for partner reading, we have talked about the challenges and unique features of decodable books—controlled vocabulary, few picture cues, simple story lines—and I keep a small basket of decodable titles in the classroom library.) Intrigued, I sit nearby to observe and listen. They flip through the stack and select *Meg* (Makar 1995), a tale about a strange, blackened creature that frightens the other characters when she approaches. Meg's identity is ultimately revealed—a hapless chicken who has fallen into the mud.

Kitty and Emma's fingers move in tandem down the page as they read the book in unison. Responsibility for reading switches back and forth, word by word or phrase by phrase, each reader contributing as she is able. They focus heavily on visual cues, and their fingers move left to right as they uncover words letter by letter, blending sounds to decode words:

Kitty	**Emma**
It ran	*It ran*
	up
to	
a dog. The dog ran.	*a dog. The dog ran.*
Juh-Juh-Juh	*Juh-Juh-Juh*
	Jen [for the word *Jan*]
Jan	
	Jan
and K-uh [for *Ken*]	*and K-uh* [for *Ken*]
Ken	
	ran to get
Dad. Dad can get	*Dad. Dad can get*
	rid
of	
it	*it.*

Kitty and Emma read slowly but steadily like this for thirty minutes, completing four more decodable texts before the bell rings for morning circle. Reluctantly, they stop, insert a bookmark into the text in progress, and stow it away until next time. They have been peer reading partners for approximately three weeks. Like many of their classmates, both girls were tentative, reluctant readers upon entering first grade. Now, only a few weeks later, peer partnerships support their sustained involvement in reading.

▪ Introducing Peer Partnerships

I begin peer partnerships on the first day of school as a way to encourage children to stay with books longer when they are reading independently. With strategizing partner at their side, students confer, reread, confirm, and adjust, enjoying all kinds of texts together. In these trusting collaborations, readers at approximately the same level feel safe taking risks, making mistakes, and trying new strategies.

For my students, these partnerships are laboratories in which to experiment, test, and refine their reading skills while really reading. Partnerships also encourage collaborative research during science and social studies projects and give children a safe context in which to try out the fluent, expressive reading I model when reading aloud and presenting shared reading lessons.

When I ask my students what they think about peer partnerships, they reveal their feelings as well as the facts: "We read one at a time—like read a book, the whole book. We go back and forth. Freddie goes first, I go second. It's kinda cool that we go one at a time 'cause it's easier for us to read separately. I read, then Freddie reads. We take turns."

Midmorning on the first day of school, I gather my students in the class-room's carpeted center area and read a picture book aloud. The book changes from year to year, but most often it's *Charlotte's Web* (White 1952), because it re-mains one of my favorite books of all time and because it is such a terrific model for building a caring classroom community. When I finish, I talk about my likes and dislikes as a reader and why *Charlotte's Web* is so dear to me. I tell them how my mother read it over and over to me until I could read it myself. I show them my worn, tattered copy of the book from the early 1950s, the front pages cov-ered with looping scribbles—my early attempts to imitate adult cursive writing long before I knew about the alphabet. We talk about the pleasures of curling up with a good book, and I invite them to tell about their favorites.

Slowly I bring the conversation around to our next activity—independent reading—when they can choose books to read and enjoy. As I try to excite them about the prospect, showing them a selection of little books, pointing out the classroom library, the book baskets, picture books displayed all over the room, invariably one small hand will go up: "What about me? I can't read yet."

This is the opening I need. I give a quick minilesson on the many aspects of reading: opening a book, reading left to right, reading the pictures and talking about the story they tell, noticing the print, reading the print, reading to the book's last page, noticing the back cover. I then suggest that they might like to do this reading with a friend. Depending on the group and the social interactions I've observed during the past hour or two, I either invite students to find book buddies or pair them up myself. As children find books and settle in, I circulate, listening, offering praise, suggesting books or strategies as needed, and support-ing in whatever ways I can.

As the weeks progress and I learn more about students' social, emotional, and academic needs, I implement more formal peer partnerships that remain to-gether for six to eight weeks. But in the beginning, partnerships are simply an extension of our reading aloud, a coming together to share books.

■ Why Use Peer Partnerships with Emergent Readers?

In my work with primary-grade teachers, I am often asked for ways to involve children in meaningful, *productive* independent reading at the beginning of the school year "when they can't read." My usual reply is that children become readers the moment they recognize that print names and conveys meaning. But I also recognize the more important questions implicit in this query: How can we encourage children to love books and reading? And how can we encourage in-dependence when reading is still so difficult?

Are partnerships right for your emergent readers? There are several things to consider:

- What purpose does social or collaborative reading have in your literacy program?

- What makes a reading partnership?

- How do children use the choice and autonomy afforded in peer partnerships to develop as readers?

Primary-grade teachers incorporate many kinds of reading into their literacy programs: teacher read-alouds; shared reading of big books, charts, and poems; guided reading; and independent reading. Teachers know how to teach and guide, how to conduct guided reading lessons, how to assess, how to instruct children regarding letters, sounds, and word solving. Teachers are also comfortable in their role as "leader": letting go is not always so easy. When children are on their own, how can teachers, as the people most responsible for their learning, be certain they are "doing it right"?

When young children read independently, they problem-solve, using their nascent understanding about what reading is to guide their thinking. Stepping into the textual worlds of print and pictures, they use their unique knowledge and background to apply, refine, and practice word analysis and comprehension skills and strategies learned through direct instruction. Putting it all together in order to read alone can be daunting. If the goal of beginning reading programs is to foster children's independence, peer partnerships provide important intermediate steps toward independence.

When one thinks of September first graders, *independent* is not the first adjective that comes to mind. In the fall of first grade, teachers demonstrate while children listen, learn, and practice. Some first graders are emergent readers, some may be even less experienced. Emergent readers as defined by Fountas and Pinnell (1996) are just beginning to control print, word-by-word matching, and directionality. Unlike in buddy reading (Samway et al., 1995), paired reading, and cross-age reading (Muldowney 1995; Nes 1997; Topping & Lindsay 1992), peer reading partners have approximately equal expertise. Although no two readers come to the printed page with identical backgrounds, experiences, and skills, research confirms that emergent readers of approximately equal expertise will "put their heads together" over text, each contributing as they are able, discussing, problem-solving, and conferring about words, sentences, meaning, and nuance as they construct text together (Griffin 2000, 2001, 2002; McGillivray 1997; McGillivray & Hawes 1994).

Most first graders thrive in social contexts, learning and growing through interactions with their peers as they read and write together. Students appreciate and treasure partner reading in emotional ways that we as adults may not fully understand: "When my friend, Art, and me are reading, it gives me a feeling that I'm his friend." Students also view partner reading as beneficial to their individual growth as readers: "It's fun and you can learn by it. I learn new words and I learn that reading is fun because you learn exciting words and you get smarter." Finally, students show their appreciation for the opportunity to read with a buddy by using this time responsibly and productively. Pairing children, then supporting these relationships over time, is an ongoing, analytic endeavor, sometimes challenging but well worth the effort.

Emergent readers "use pictures to support meaning and rely on language as a strong cueing system" (Fountas & Pinnell 1996, p. 177), but often these cueing strategies are not enough as they struggle to put the pieces together alone. For emergent readers, independent reading is often more enjoyable and successful when they have a collaborator at their side. The use of language and pictures is evident in the following interaction between Bobby and Pete as they read *The Biggest Cake in the World* (Cowley 1988).

Bobby	Pete
Mrs. Delicious got a . . . [pauses on *tractor*]	
	[Points to the picture of the tractor] *tr-tr-tr-tractor.*
tractor to cut [for *pull*] *the*	
	[Points] *p-p-pull*
[Nods] *pull the biggest cake in the world.*	
[Turns page]	
Mrs. Delicious	*Mrs. Delicious.*
got a . . . [pauses on *chainsaw*]	
[Together, Bobby and Pete study the picture]	
chainsaw	
to cut the biggest cake in the world.	*to cut the biggest cake in the world.*

Again and again, these partners use text patterns to support their reading. Encountering unfamiliar multisyllabic words like *tractor* and *chainsaw*, they rely heavily on illustrations to decipher the message. Illustrations, text, discussion, and the presence of a collaborator provide the support both readers need to be successful with this predictable, highly patterned story.

Research suggests that peer partnerships help beginning readers become more self-sufficient and less reliant on the teacher for assistance (Rhodes & Shanklin 1993; Griffin 2000). When children work together, they view their peers as "collaborators in a joint enterprise rather than competitors for the teacher's [attention and] approval" (Barnes 1992, p. 109). Collaborators compensate "for each other's blind spots" (Olby 1970, p. 963). When young children read, there are many blind spots—unknown words, confusing language, misinterpretations of text. Even the structure of books may be blinding, unfamiliar territory for the beginning reader. Approximately equal expertise does not mean the same expertise. Shoulder to shoulder, peer partners walk together through unfamiliar landscapes, pooling their resources in order to read and enjoy all kinds of text.

In the interaction below, Kitty and Bobby read *Mr. Grump* (Cowley 1987). As peer partners of approximately equal expertise, they share the role of the capable peer as they work diligently to take their respective needs and preferences into account:

Kitty	**Bobby**
Who growled at the . . . [pauses on *mail*]	
	[Leans closer] *mail.*
mail . . . carrier.	
Mr. Grump. Mr. Grump. Mr.	*Mr. Grump. Mr. Grump. Mr. Grump-grump-grump*
Who mailed [substitutes *mailed* for *growled,*	
sits back, shakes her head]	
who growled . . . at the milk carrier.	[Whispers] *growled.*
Mr. Grump. Mr. Grump.	*who growled . . . at the milk carrier.*
Mr. Grump-grump-grump.	*Mr. Grump. Mr. Grump.*
	Mr. Grump-grump-grump.

They continue reading chorally until the end of the story. Although Kitty leads, the role of capable peer, rather than being fixed, continually shifts from one learner to the other.

■ Building Community Through Reading Partnerships

In many classrooms, the lines are blurred between home and school as children talk about reading as something you do not only at school but everywhere: "My favorite partner is my next-door neighbor. Then in school, it's Rob and Nat, 'cause they like me and I like them." For many children reading alone and in partnership is a natural extension of life, not something imposed or required. They clearly love to read, and in reading they learn about themselves and the world while sitting shoulder to shoulder with a buddy: "I like to read with my grandfather because he talks to me and I love him very much. I like to read with Ms. Vito and Connor, because he's very nice and a nice friend to have."

Reading partnerships establish literate connections in a trusting family of learners. Partnerships begin or deepen relationships centered around text. These relationships carry over into their interactions during literature discussions and other collaborative pursuits.

FIG. 1–1

It is the start of partner reading and Emma and Lottie are perched atop a fake stuffed tiger. Lottie sits on the head of the tiger, Emma on its back. The partners are reading Lottie's selection, *Look! I Can Read!* (Hood 2000):

Lottie	**Emma**
bumble bee [for the word *bee*]	
	No! [points] *bee.*
bee.	
I can [for *wrote*]	*I can* [for *wrote*]
	No!
	I know [for *wrote*]
	[Points at the word *bedtime*] This one's hard.
[Nods] I know.	
	[Together, they study the word]
bet [for *bedtime*]	
	[Points] *bed . . . bedtime*

Although Lottie takes the lead here, both readers contribute throughout. When Emma and Lottie complete the book, it is Emma's turn to select a book; she chooses *The Pencil* (Randell 1996). Without a word, the partners switch places, so that Emma is now sitting on the tiger's head. *The Pencil* is a short, patterned story in which the pencil draws each animal as it is introduced. The animals ask questions such as "Where is my tail?" In response, the pencil draws the tail and answers, "Here it is."

This is a familiar book for both readers, and Emma reads while Lottie looks over her shoulder, her eyes following along. Emma reads pages 2 and 3 correctly, then says, "Pencils can't talk! Or dogs can't talk!" She then reads pages 4 and 5 correctly and says, "Pencils could definitely not talk!" They continue to read through the story, discussing illustrations and making plans to draw some of the animals later.

Emma and Lottie have developed a comfortable, structured context within which they read and enjoy books together. The switch in positions from the tiger's head to its back occurs each time a reader selects a new book. The girl perched on the tiger's head leads, her partner helping and assisting as needed. Switching seats—which peer partners commonly do—enables them to devote their full attention to the task of reading. During forty-five minutes, Lottie and Emma read seven books, pausing from time to time to discuss pictures, characters, and stories. They spend five minutes selecting new books; the rest of the time they are engaged in and involved with reading.

When beginning readers negotiate their way through text, the different capacities and strengths they bring to the shared task of reading are revealed. "Collaboration operates through a process in which the successful intellectual achievements of one person arouse the intellectual passions and enthusiasms of others, and through the fact that what was first expressed only by one individual becomes a common intellectual possession instead of fading away into isolation" (Olby 1970, p. 963). This is a beautiful description of how primary-grade peer partners work, arousing the passions and interests of one another, sharing a thought, an idea, a book, or a project, their common intellectual ownership becoming an integral part of their learning.

As adults we read in soft chairs, beds, or other spots where we feel comfortable and can give ourselves over to the pleasure of it. No one tells us "Sit here" or "Don't sit there." As literate individuals, we decide what works best for us. Young readers deserve the same freedom to choose and develop structures and frameworks that suit them as individuals and partners.

■ Beginning Peer Partnerships at Midyear

Christine Wiltshire and Sarah Rich each teach first grade in an urban charter school in its second year of operation. By January literacy routines and structures are well established, and these teachers decide to try peer partnerships for the first time.

Christine views partner reading as valuable time for students to practice the skills and strategies she has modeled during shared reading, guided reading, and reading minilessons. "Buddy reading builds students' confidence, and they're verbalizing strategies so that they remember them when reading on their own." When students are paired with peers, Christine observes that they make "much better use of sustained silent reading—they're more involved with a buddy, they're engaged and enthusiastic."

Sarah observes that partner reading gives children time to practice and "gain better control of concepts about print as they discuss books together." She also believes that partner reading promotes good listening and "encourages children to work together."

Learning from Christine and Her Students

All of Christine's students are excited about partner reading, something they see as a welcome change from their routine of solo reading during sustained silent reading. As Briana says, "It's fun, and sometimes I get a little help. We get to read interesting books."

Christine articulates simple, clear expectations for partner reading: sit side by side, read the same book, take turns, and use quiet voices. She also expects partners to help each other and tells them, "Do what I would do. Hint, don't tell, if your partner is stuck on a word." Hinting strategies she emphasizes are:

- Look at the first letter and say the sound, then wait to see if your partner can say the word.

- Ask your partner what would make sense.

- Look at the picture.

- Reread the sentence together.

- Help your partner look for a familiar "chunk."

After children hint and wait, Christine encourages them to tell the word so that reading can move forward. Even though they are new to partnerships and the language of collaboration, when interviewed, Christine's students echo these strategies again and again.

Christine does not specify how children should take turns, allowing the partners to make these decisions. She has observed them reading productively in three ways: chorally, alternating pages, and reading whole books to each other. Soon, she plans to collaborate with students to create a chart listing expectations for partners. She also plans to begin discussions and minilessons highlighting collaborative partner reading behavior.

Finding time in which to partner-read and providing "just-right" books for peer partners are challenges for Christine. Her school is in its second year of operation, and classroom leveled-book collections are small. After observing partnerships for several weeks, Christine realizes that students need to "refresh" their reading boxes (vertical files filled with books) so that the books they bring with them to partner reading are "just right" and not too difficult.

Learning from Sarah and Her Students

During the first weeks of implementation, Sarah decides to use partner reading to build students' comprehension skills and deepen their appreciation and understanding of text. To that end, she asks partners to retell stories together, paying particular attention to "the beginning, middle, and end of stories." Additionally, Sarah instructs partners to discuss characters, comparing and contrasting character traits and motivations. She supports students' comprehension strategies by modeling and using picture cards and questions during minilessons.

In Sarah's room, two students, Lynn and Ruth, sit side by side in the cozy library corner, in a cocoon of pillows. Pillows, books, and shelving muffle the hum of the classroom. Lynn holds the book while Ruth points. They read chorally with expression, smiling and laughing, totally immersed in their task. Later, both children tell me that they like buddy reading because it's fun. Lynn also tells me she prefers to read with a partner rather than alone, because "your buddy says maybe you did a good job or not—you kind of like your partner for that."

When I talk with Sarah's students, their responses suggest that they view reading as a task that can be accomplished using step-by-step procedures, special tools, and the expertise of others: "When you don't know words and they do, they can help you solve the problem."

Sarah's students are accustomed to reading independently every day during sustained silent reading, and they appreciate this new collaborative kind of reading for the opportunity it gives them to apply and test strategies as they build

FIG. 1–2 *Partner reading*

text together: "I just tell 'em to stretch it out like a rubber band and try all the sounds."

Sarah's students view reading as problem solving, and this attitude, fostered by Sarah's teaching, helps them plunge into partnership reading with deliberation and a spirit of adventure. They also appreciate and love the chance to read together, rather than alone: "It's so fun. I get to learn the words that are tricky. When I read by myself I get lonely."

Sarah supports partner collaborations by giving students specific directions about postreading activities like discussing characters and retelling the story. Strategies stressed in Sarah's reading minilessons often find their way into partner interactions. Sarah expresses surprise and delight at observing children using "tricky-word cards" (a tool to remind them of word-solving strategies) and other strategies to help each other during partner reading. Like Christine, Sarah sees the need for more books. She also states that "There are some children who I don't think get it," adding that some students are having a hard time with partner reading.

Recommendations for Beginning Peer Partnerships Midyear

Like most classroom practices, partner reading should be viewed as a process that we refine and smooth with time. Once implemented, we cannot necessarily expect these relationships to run smoothly without teacher invention and support. Children need models of collaboration and structures to help them feel safe and clear about their tasks.

Pairing
Both Christine and Sarah assign student partners, checking in frequently to make sure relationships are supportive and friendly. Children may occasionally choose partners on their own.

Moving from individual reading to reading with a partner
At midyear, Christine and Sarah agree that children are accustomed to independent reading but do not always use their time productively. When paired with a strategizing partner during independent reading, however, students read longer and, as Syd suggests, are better able to attend to the task: "When I read with a buddy, it's kinda fun; when I read something alone, I get sleeping, but with a buddy, I read another book!"

Modeling strategies that help partners "think like readers"
Both Christine and Sarah have expectations for partner behavior, and their children strive hard to meet them: "We listen to Ms. Wiltshire. When she finishes, we read. We take turns."

In addition to high expectations, both Christine and Sarah trust students to structure their interactions and, for the most part, children do indeed organize and structure their time responsibly: "We go to a quiet corner, look at the position of each other, and that's how we decide who goes first. Then we read."

To support students' efforts, both teachers make their own reading/thinking processes visible through "think-alouds" and focused minilessons. As in most primary classrooms, students are surrounded with print. Although these particular classrooms need more leveled books, children are resourceful and find reading materials everywhere. They read print on the walls; they reread the books they have published themselves; and they reread familiar texts from browsing boxes, teacher read-alouds, and shared reading.

Extending What We Do in Peer Partnerships

It's all about practice. It's a great way for kids to read independently during centers and a wonderful way to start the day.

—Cheryl Feeney, literacy specialist

On a morning in early October, Sharon Roberts gathers her students on the rug. She distributes paper puppets of a duck and chick that the children have constructed the day before, along with individual copies of *The Chick and the Duckling* (Ginsberg 1972), to each reading partnership. She explains that partners are to reread the story, each reader portraying one of the characters. Then they are to switch parts and reread the book a second time. Finally, they are to retell the story using puppets.

Before sending students off to read, Sharon leads a short focused review of responsible partner behavior:

Sharon: What happens when your partner doesn't know a word?
Eddie: Help them say it.
Sally: Think about what makes sense.
Sharon: Yes, help them say it and think about what makes sense. Those are great strategies.
Tamara: You could look for a little word in the big word.
Sharon: Yes!
Joey: Use the word wall.
Patrick: Look at pictures and do what makes sense.

Sharon praises the children's "great strategy thinking," repeats the directions, and sends partners off to find a seat. The reading and retelling of *The Chick and the Duckling* takes about twenty minutes.

Eddie and Patrick sit side by side at a table, each holding a copy of *The Chick and the Duckling*. Eddie asks, "What do you wanta be?"

Patrick replies, "I want to be squawk–squawk–squawk." Eddie squawks in response, and the boys spend a minute playing with their puppets, making them dance, the popsicle sticks rapping a steady beat on the table. Finally, Patrick says, "I read chick, you read duck."

"Okay."

At this point, Patrick's chick becomes detached from its popsicle stick. Eddie jumps up and snatches a glue stick from a supply shelf for a quick repair. At last, all is ready and they begin. Eddie says, "The first part is the chick part." He points to the floor. "We have to use this as water. Don't start!" He flips ahead. "Yes! I'm on page 10!"

Patrick points to the first page of text. "No, you gotta read this." With that, the boys read through the story, each taking his part. They read the familiar, patterned story without miscue, using high squeaky voices and a lot of animated puppet behavior. At one point, Patrick's chick taps hard on the table and he cries, "Ow, I broke my leg," but otherwise they read without interruption until the end.

Switching parts, they begin again, each taking his part on a particular page. On page five, the text reads: "The duckling came out of the shell. 'I am out,' he said." Patrick reads "The duckling," then miscues, reading *come* for *came*.

Eddie shouts, *"Came!"*

Patrick continues reading: *". . . came out of the shell. 'I am out,' he said."* They read without further miscue until they reach the end of the story. On one page, Patrick reads text, then adds, "Beep, beep, beep," tapping and dancing his chick puppet across the table.

When they finish, they prepare to switch parts again and read the book a third time. Sharon intervenes, reminding them that they should now retell the story. Patrick says, "I'll talk about the beginning. You'll talk about the middle. I'll talk about the end, okay?" They begin retelling, using puppets to reenact the story.

Reading the characters' lines and acting out the parts using puppets help Patrick, Eddie, and their classmates step into the book. The classroom becomes the book's setting, as Eddie imagines the floor as water in which the duckling can swim. The puppets are important props, increasing the children's enjoyment and involvement in the rereading and retelling. For Patrick and Eddie, this reading of

The Chick and the Duckling isn't static, one-dimensional, or arduous, but a joyous, interactive experience in which they live the story while building fluency.

■ Using Partner Reading

Like many teachers, Sharon Roberts has a number of specific purposes and intentions for peer partner reading, and they change with every year and each unique group of children. The year I visited her classroom, she had a group of children who really needed to learn how to collaborate. Peer partner reading was a structured, purposeful way to develop productive collaborative relationships.

Sharon views peer partner reading first of all as valuable practice: rereading familiar stories helps her children read more fluently. "I still get a chance to stop in and hear children read without it being round robin [oral] reading." She also sees partner reading as a time to focus on comprehension. "This year I have built a lot of my comprehension and retelling strategies into partner reading, more so than in the past." In addition to a consistent focus on retelling events in the correct sequence, Sharon asks students to discuss literary elements such as characters, setting, and plot. She might also ask partners to create a scene depicting what might happen next, complete a story map, discuss a character's motivations or the story's problem and solution, or enact a character (as Patrick and Eddie did with their duckling and chick puppets). Sharon says, "I really want to help children build the criteria for success by articulating what makes a good retelling, a compelling plot, or interesting characters."

In implementing peer partnerships at the beginning of year, Sharon provides a lot of structure so that children will be successful. Some of these structures include:

● Asking partners to reread familiar stories they know well.

● Specifying how partners will read (in unison or separately) and giving directions about taking turns (alternating pages or taking the part of a specific character).

● Clearly outlining her expectations for partners' activities before, during, and after reading.

Structures like these enable partners to be independent and to use this time productively. "When I kneel down [to listen to partners read] and they know I'm there, what interests me is how they don't turn to me if they get stuck. They don't rely on me. They rely on their partners."

As the year goes on and children demonstrate responsible, independent be-havior, Sharon releases responsibility to students, allowing them greater auton-omy in selecting books and taking turns. "I find that structure is essential in the beginning, if I want them to use the time wisely and independently, but then I need to let go."

Peer partnerships complement and enhance all facets of a primary literacy program, providing students with time to practice skills and strategies introduced during teacher read-alouds, shared reading, word-solving lessons, and guided and independent reading. When reading alone, beginning readers often become tired or a little "frayed around the edges" (Collins, in Calkins 2001); however, when they are shoulder to shoulder with a strategizing partner, children linger longer over books, supporting and assisting each other as they construct text together.

When implementing peer partnerships as part of your literacy program, ask:

- How can I make connections between other aspects of my literacy pro-gram and peer partnerships?

- What are my purposes, goals, and intentions for peer partnerships?

- What can I learn from children?

Educators are constantly seeking ways to move children toward indepen-dence, gradually turning the responsibility for learning over to their students (Pearson & Gallagher 1983). Fountas and Pinnell (1996) describe this transfer of responsibility as moving from activities characterized by a great deal of teacher support and control and little student control to activities characterized by little teacher support and a lot of student control. In peer partnerships, much of the responsibility for reading is the students'; this helps learners move from the supportive context of guided reading toward the ultimate goal of reading independently.

■ The Place of Partner Reading in the Learning Continuum

Many kinds of literacy activities take place throughout the school day. Figure 2.1 arranges the most common ones along a continuum from activities character-ized as highly teacher controlled to those in which most or all control rests with students. The list of activities is by no means inclusive, and you will no doubt have other strategies and activities to add. Nevertheless, it is a starting point for thinking about how we move readers toward independence through the struc-tures and strategies we introduce.

Activities characterized by:
High teacher support & involvement
High teacher control
Low student involvement
Low student control

Activities characterized by:
Low teacher support & involvement
Low teacher control
High student involvement
High student control

JOINT RESPONSIBILITY

←——————————————————————————————→

Activities with high teacher control include:

Direct instruction
Modeling
Teacher demonstrations
Teacher read-alouds
Teacher-led discussions

Activities in which teachers and students share responsibility include:

Shared reading
Shared writing
Modeled writing
Interactive writing
Scaffolded reading
Student demonstrations
Student modeling
Guided reading
Structured writing

Activities with high student control include:

Peer partner reading
Independent reading
Independent writing

FIG. 2–1 *Continuum of literacy learning*

Along the continuum of literacy learning, peer partnerships fall to the right and are characterized by a high level of student responsibility. Although partners may receive support, guidance, and occasional redirection from teachers, the children are largely in control of the task and decide how they will read. In addition, peer partnerships are connected to and can enhance different types of literacy activities no matter where they fall along the continuum.

Teacher Read-Alouds

Most primary-grade teachers read aloud to children several times during the school day, choosing from a variety of picture books and simple chapter books. These read-alouds may relate to science, social studies, or literary themes. As teachers read, they pause to ask children to predict, draw conclusions, or make inferences about what has been read. During or after reading, teachers ask students to discuss characters' motivations or feelings. These modeled literate conversations can then be carried over into peer partnerships as children read and discuss books in pairs or small groups.

Reading aloud builds literate classroom communities. By sharing a story and laughing, crying, or sighing over a character's journey, students and teachers come together as people who trust and care about each other. This trust, along with shared enjoyment, sets up the context for collaborative, trusting peer partnerships. As first-grade teacher Kristen Vito says, "We build relationships and community by sharing literature together. Building community leads to success. It's the key ingredient, whether it's discussing books together as a whole group, getting behavior and strategies under control, or working in pairs."

Shared Reading

Shared reading, in the center of the continuum, invites children to take a more active role in the reading process. The behavior teachers model and discuss when reading big books, chart stories, and poems together with their students is reflected in partners' behavior: pointing to letters whose sounds need to be blended, word-by-word matching, and covering part or all of a word and guessing what would make sense. Following their teacher's lead, peer partners use punctuation and capitalization to respect sentence boundaries in order to read meaningfully. As first-grader Emma says, "We read like we're the character. We want to get it right, like the character thinks, and those marks [periods and exclamation points] help us."

Guided Reading

Students assume greater control during guided reading. Although teachers introduce the text, each child reads the entire text, guided and supported by both

FIG. 2–2 *Circle of readers*

teacher and peers. The reader retains control of the task but is supported throughout by the direct teaching of important strategies before, during, and after reading. For beginning readers, peer partnerships are important bridges between teacher-supported guided reading and totally independent reading. Teachers expect children to use the behavior they learn about during guided reading when they read with their partner and when they read alone.

Independent Reading

Independent reading is always the ultimate goal. When reading independently in books they have chosen, children practice the skills their teachers have modeled and taught through direct instruction. Some teachers, and I am among them, begin the year partnering students during reading workshop, believing they will read longer and enjoy "independent reading" more if they have a strategizing partner at their side, a partner of approximately equal expertise who will not dominate but help build their understanding.

Heads together, fingers pressed to the page, peer partners share their expertise, the control of the task continually shifting back and forth. Peer partners rereading familiar text linger longer and notice details about print, characters, and stories that may have eluded them on a first or second reading. Partners notice and discuss language structures like word and sentence patterns, and they make connections between print and illustrations. Armed with strategies they have practiced and made their own during partner reading, independent readers feel more confident about selecting just-right books, problem solving when they encounter challenges, and reading expressively and exuberantly.

Word Solving

An emergent reader's efforts to solve an unfamiliar word are visible, whether he or she is working alone or helping a partner. Emergent readers have not yet acquired a vast store of words they recognize "on sight" and are still learning, practicing, and refining decoding strategies. If you ask an emergent reader "What makes reading hard?" more often than not she or he will say something like "not knowing the words" or "hard words."

Peer partnerships are ideal contexts in which readers can practice and refine the word-solving skills and strategies teachers have taught through modeling and direct instruction. If I ask children what they do to help partners, their answer often centers upon helping a partner who is "stuck on a word." I then encourage students to share with their partner the strategies that work for them.

Literate Discussion

In describing the kinds of scaffolding and support they offer to their partners, Sharon Roberts' students mention many kinds of strategies. Some are related to word solving, like "tell the word" or "look for a cluster." Others relate to collaboration and how to be a supportive presence for one's partner, like "take turns" or "use your strategies and help your partner to use hers."

Sharon's students' ease in discussing the many strategies they use attests to the literate context of this classroom. Expectations for first graders are clear. Sharon structures each lesson carefully and gives explicit directions. This enables children to accomplish reading tasks comfortably and responsibly. The transition into partner reading always includes a discussion and/or review of responsible partner behavior. A chart on the wall, created with the children, lists expectations, and Sharon often refers to it:

1. Use quiet reading voices.
2. Be sure both partners read.
3. Follow along.
4. Help your partner when needed.

Sharon is clear and precise in communicating her expectations, and her students respond in kind. She trusts the children and takes her cues from them,

FIG. 2–3

designing the kinds of structure and support they need to be successful. At the same time, she knows when to step away and give partners more choice and freedom. "Very seldom do I see a child so upset with a partner that I need to intervene. I think they have a way to communicate with each other that they don't need me to know."

Teachers do not and cannot know everything about children's interactions and communications. In fact, some of students' most creative pursuits may fall below a teacher's radar screen. Therefore, structuring carefully, then stepping back, may be some of the most important "teaching" if the goal is to help young children toward independence as readers. For young readers just beginning to control print, reading can be slow, risky business. Sharon is sensitive to and aware of children's vulnerabilities. Her careful structuring helps children feel secure in peer partnerships.

The Reading–Writing Connection

Jenny Baumeister calls her students to the circle area and explains that she will be writing a descriptive paragraph about a subject that interests her and that she "knows a lot about"—camels—and that later in the day they will write their own descriptive paragraph about something they know a lot about. First, Jenny shares her notes about camels, which she calls her "planning page," a list of words and phrases on chart paper: *desert, humps, tan fur, eyelashes, long time no water.* Then she leads the group in a short, focused discussion about camels in which the children contribute their ideas. At one point the group wonders why camels sometimes have one hump or two and a boy says, "One hump means that they're still little." Jenny praises his thinking, then explains that there are different kinds of camels that live in different parts of the world, some with one hump, some with two. Finally, she begins writing using the facts they have generated to structure the piece. Children help with the wording of sentences.

Facts About Camels

Camels are desert animals. They can have one hump or two. Camels are big mammals. They can be male or female. The camel's fur is tannish yellow like a leprechaun's treasure. The camel's eyelashes are so long that sand doesn't get in their eyes during a sandstorm. Did you know that camels can go a long time without water? Would you want to be a camel?

Following this modeled writing lesson, students prepare to work with new reading partners. Jenny reminds them of responsible partner behavior—they need to share, take turns, and read the same book—and partners disperse to choose books from the guided reading collection. This takes several minutes.

Jenny's paragraph has introduced a new writing genre: description. Before this lesson, these first graders had been writing personal narratives, procedural pieces, letters, reading responses, and poetry. Jenny tells me that modeled writing "is really big in our school this year." In fact, teachers have recently completed a twelve-week literacy course taught by the building principal with modeled writing as its centerpiece. Modeled writing examples are everywhere in the classrooms, on walls, ceilings, doors, and easels.

Jenny does not specify that the children read nonfiction, but some, like Allie and Helen, select nonfiction texts on a variety of science and social studies topics. Allie and Helen sit catty-corner to each other at a table sharing the book *Spikes, Scales, and Armor* (Windsor 1999), reading alternate pages. Each time they switch, they swivel the book to face the reader.

Helen	Allie
	[Points to the picture of a hermit crab] I could write about these. My friend has one of these. I know a lot about 'em.

[On page 6, the text reads, *Some animals have scales. The scales help to keep them safe.*]

Some animals have . . . schools [for *scales*]

           sc–sc–ales.

scales. The scales help to keep them safe.

[On page 8, the text reads, *The armadillo has scales. It can roll into a ball to keep safe.*]

This [for *the*]

      The [pauses and points to *the;* then gazes from picture to print] *armadillo! The armadillo has scales. It can roll into a ball to keep safe.*

[Together, Helen and Allie read several pages chorally. Aside from one instance where they ask me for the word *pangolin,* they read without miscue, pausing occasionally to discuss words or pictures. They come to page 13.]

      This bird has armor on its . . . hurd [for *head*]

[Points at the word, then points to her head and shrugs]
Head!

      Head! This bird has armor on its head. The armor keeps the bird's head safe.

Helen and Allie's conversation reveals their thinking and planning as readers and writers. Following modeled writing with peer reading partnerships connects the processes of reading and writing for children. As partners share and discuss nonfiction texts, they are also planning their descriptive writing pieces. Inviting her students into her writing process as active participants, Jenny uses her interest in and thinking about camels as a model they can carry over into their own literate pursuits.

Even though their classroom library is small, Jenny's students have many opportunities to interact with continuous written text, thanks in large part to the print-rich environment created through modeled writing. These young readers and writers are surrounded by written text that reflects their interests and aspirations, their thoughts about historic figures, and their factual descriptions of the natural world.

Jenny's first graders are accustomed to collaborating during modeled writing. "Buddy reading" is one more way they can work together, sharing and building text word by word, sentence by sentence, page by page. They appreciate this time and use it to learn about themselves and the world: "I never knew Kurt knew about that stuff or knew that book so well. He's very funny." As veteran collaborators, they often answer my question about why they prefer to read with a partner as Valerie does: "'Cause I don't like to be alone." They respect each other's literate thinking, and they appreciate the unexpected joys of working together: "I was surprised she was reading this book, because it looked so hard. I liked that!"

3 | Organizing the Classroom for Successful Reader Collaboration

Anne Santoro gathers her students on the carpet for "centers time." It is midmorning on Tuesday, the second day these center activities are being offered, and Anne takes five minutes to review procedures. As she talks, she asks two students assigned to the writing and ABC centers to set up those materials. They retrieve the appropriate tubs from a shelf, lay the contents out on one of the classroom worktables, and return to the carpet. Anne completes her introductory remarks, and children disperse to one of four centers—poetry, listening, writing, or ABC—and work quietly and independently. As children work, Anne circulates, conferring with groups and individuals. When children complete their center activity, they clean up their materials, retrieve book bags, find a buddy, and partner-read for the remainder of the period.

Anne's communication of her expectations for independent work builds a responsible community of learners. Whether the students are reading, writing, or setting up a center, they work competently and confidently, are considerate of one another, and demonstrate that they are aware of themselves as independent learners. When Anne asks children to buddy-read, their well-developed interpersonal and independent skills enable them to support each other collaboratively and responsibly.

Classroom environment is a key component in encouraging successful, effective peer partnerships. Taking time to build a trusting, responsible classroom community supports all teaching and learning pursuits. When planning and creating literate environments, teachers should whenever possible turn over responsibility to students. Inviting children to help create the spaces in which they will work, learn, and teach encourages them to take more active roles in all classroom activities and brings them into the environment as full and active participants in the learning process.

How to organize space and materials, when to begin reading partnerships, and where reading partnerships fit in the overall school day are important considerations. A few of the questions we need to ask ourselves when planning space conducive to effective peer partnerships are:

- How can we design an environment that supports student responsibility and independence?

- What kinds of spaces support collaborations during peer partner reading?

- How can we organize classroom and materials to support effective partnerships?

- What tools do partners need when collaborating to decode text?

■ Creating Literate Spaces

We further children's learning in myriad ways when we ask them to help plan and implement the tools, materials, and spaces that then nurture them as literate individuals. Trusting classroom communities make ideal contexts in which peer partnerships can flourish, and they should include reading spaces that enhance and encourage collaboration. Partners need comfortable spaces in which to read and discuss books. After observing my own first graders and hundreds of others, I have learned that what is comfortable for one reading partnership may be uncomfortable for another. My rule about reading spaces, for both partnership and solo reading, is simple: readers can sit anywhere in the classroom as long as they stay focused on reading and book discussion. Some of the places in which I have observed peer partners reading over the years include:

- sitting or lying on comfortable couches, sofas, armchairs, and rocking chairs

- sitting or lying surrounded by pillows, large and small, in book corners or library nooks

FIG. 3–1

- sitting or lying in a clearly defined "buddy reading center," usually a small corner of the room furnished with cushions or pillows

- sitting side by side or catty-corner at desks and tables (some partners really prefer flat, hard surfaces for book handling and sharing)

- sitting or lying on carpeted surfaces in the classroom

- perched atop a fake stuffed tiger rug

- sitting or lying under tables or desks, including the teacher's desk (a favorite spot in my first-grade classroom)

- standing at the window, singing books to the birds

- strolling, pointers in hand, reading charts and other print around the room

The most important thing about space is what children do in it. Reading is a deeply personal activity. As readers, we all deserve to choose where we will read. If partners are engaged and involved with books and reading, then they are most likely situated in a space that works for them. Some readers like to be out in the open in plain sight for all to see, and others like privacy or the thrill of "hiding out" when they read. Some prefer cozy, comfortable spots, while others like neat, orderly spaces. As in so many other aspects of classroom life, we need to trust children to find the spaces most appropriate for them.

A few reminders about partner spaces:

- Take time to discuss with students how to use spaces responsibly during partner reading.

- Allow partners to choose where they will sit as long as they use the space responsibly.

- Provide many inviting spaces in the classroom where partners can curl up with a book:

  - reading nooks with soft pillows and cushions
  - carpeted library and circle areas with throw pillows, beanbag chairs, and stuffed animals
  - tables, desks, and other flat surfaces
  - classroom lofts, the space under tables, hallway areas, wherever partners can get comfortable and stay involved with their reading

■ Organizing the Classroom and Materials

If we want children to make good choices about reading materials, our classroom collections need to be well organized and easy to access. In many classrooms, peer partners select books from "browsing boxes" that contain books just right for them. In other rooms, students have individual book bags from which

FIG. 3–2 *Browsing boxes*

to select reading books. Still others choose freely from library shelves, browsing carefully to find books at a level that is just right for them.

My recommendations for organizing classroom and materials include the following:

- Develop a clear, user-friendly system for organizing books and materials.

- Enlist children's help in taking care of libraries and book collections.

- Establish clear routines for book bags, baskets, or other personal book containers to help students use them effectively.

- Whenever possible, make connections between school and home reading:
  - Send books and other materials home regularly.
  - Make your expectations regarding these materials clear to parents and caregivers.

Classroom Libraries

Literate societies prize their libraries. Libraries should, therefore, be at the heart of every school and every classroom. Our youngest readers need rich and varied libraries from which to choose books for solo and partner reading.

There are many books for teachers about setting up and maintaining classroom libraries, leveled book collections, and browsing boxes. Fountas and Pinnell's *Guided Reading: Good First Teaching for All Children* (1996) and *Matching Books to Readers: Using Leveled Books in Guided Reading, K–3* (1999) are excellent resources in planning room and library setup to establish child-friendly collections.

Along with access to rich, user-friendly libraries of books, students also need instruction on how to use libraries. Important considerations for me in establishing and maintaining library and leveled collections with students follow.

- Establish procedures for finding, selecting, and introducing books.

- Establish procedures for returning books to shelves and baskets so that the books remain invitingly accessible to all.

- Refresh collections throughout the year to include new books from the school's literacy closet, my personal collection, and local libraries.

- Talk about and model how to select and read widely, so that students sometimes move out of their "comfort level" if a topic or story is of interest.

Book Storage: Bags, Baskets, and Files

Many teachers ask children to select books for partner or individual reading before reading workshop or reading time and set them aside in individual book baskets or other containers. Some teachers specify that children select the books from leveled browsing boxes. Others allow more latitude, including classroom library shelves, baskets of decodable texts, poetry, "author of the month" baskets, and nonfiction collections relative to topics currently being studied across the curriculum.

Some teachers ask children to keep book selections in their desks or cubbies, and others provide special containers for independent or partner reading books. Possible "book containers" for students' independent book selections include:

- vertical files (cardboard or plastic)

- book baskets and boxes (cardboard or plastic)

- book bags (self-sealing plastic food storage bags or cloth bags closed with zippers, Velcro, or a drawstring)

- two-pocket folders (a little unwieldy when storing more than one or two books, but handy for storing book logs, response journals, and reading reminders)

Containers ensure that reading materials are available and organized when readers need them. As Ike says, "We drop books out of the bag, then we pick one. We all read together." Children appreciate these tools and use them to organize and structure their peer reading. Although teachers get the ball rolling, partners develop routines and structures far beyond our directions, using tools effectively to begin reading. Here Rosie explains the routine she has developed with her partner:

> First we get our books from our basket and then we take the books out of the bag that's in the basket. Then we put the books in order. We need them in order to start reading. Then somebody gets a turn. We read the title of the book, and then we go through all the story until we get to the end. Then we choose another book from the pile.

Two final considerations about book containers follow.

First, rereading and practice are important, but students' individual book selections also need to change, and change often, if we want children to progress as independent readers. When she wants her first graders to select new books for their reading files, Christine Wiltshire announces that it's "time to refresh," a signal for them to reshelf most of the books in their cardboard vertical files and select new ones. Refreshing our reading material keeps us fresh as readers, ensures that we are always exploring new texts, building on our prior experiences. Refreshing material does not mean that children shouldn't be allowed to revisit well-loved books, of course, but we also want to encourage students to stretch their reading muscles.

Second, many teachers send book bags home, affording children one more chance to reread and practice these familiar texts. Reading at home has always been a critical aspect of my literacy program. Once or twice a week, my first graders take home a WEB book—a "wonderfully exciting book," a term borrowed from Regie Routman (2000)—to read to family members. These are books they have read during partner or independent reading. Accompanying the book is an optional comment sheet, on which family members may give feedback about children's reading or ask questions. Typically, comment sheets come back to school filled with questions at the start of the year then taper off as the months go by and children grow and develop as readers.

Some teachers tell me they cannot send books home because they will never get them back. Although I would like to believe that if we teach responsibility this will be less of a problem, the reality of busy and complicated lives means that sometimes books do get lost. There are, however, many ways to send print materials home for children to share with families. I often send children's illustrated copies of poems, language experience work, and chart stories. I also encourage families to visit and use public libraries. Some teachers and schools invest in KEEP books (published by The Ohio State Literacy Collaborative), inexpensive consumable books for children to keep. Additionally, many reading series now have reproducible copies of little books and stories that children can take home to read and share. Finally, teachers can publish children's writing, then send these original works home, thereby providing the most meaningful texts of all for young readers.

■ Providing Tools for Peer Partners

Much like carpenters use tools to build houses and furniture, partners use tools to build stories together. Like all reader scaffolds, the most relevant or useful tools are created with children's assistance, not simply handed to them. Tools that children create themselves are often the first they pull out when they need reading support.

Whenever I introduce a reading or writing routine or strategy, I model or demonstrate, then invite children's participation. For example, after routines are established, I encourage children to propose and construct words for the word wall and other classroom word collections (compound words, homonyms, palindromes, and so on). I also invite them to make bookmarks, charts, and written reminders about helpful reading habits. I listen carefully, and when they suggest a tool I haven't thought of, I encourage them to construct it and make it available for their peers.

I often suggest partners use one of the following tools to enhance and support their collaborations:

1. *Strategy gloves,* each finger outlining a different reading or partner strategy. These gloves can be constructed using:

   - white canvas carpentry gloves
   - rubber gloves
   - paper gloves, laminated as an entity for children to hold or laminated directly onto reading tables or other surfaces

2. *Word frames.* Word frames help readers zero in on words as they work to decode them. Word frames are also very useful tools in focusing partners' attention so that they can better help each other. Frames can be purchased through educational catalogues or constructed of cardboard or soft but rigid plastic sheeting.

FIG. 3–3 *Strategy gloves and word frame*

3. *Tricky-word cards.* Create and laminate cards outlining strategies for readers to use when encountering unknown words. Such cards are useful whenever and wherever children are reading. Partner-specific strategies can be included.

4. *Strategy bookmarks.* Young readers love bookmarks, especially those they create themselves. In *Snapshots* (2000), Linda Hoyt suggests making "fix it" bookmarks to remind readers of important strategies (she provides blank templates on pages 20 and 205). Bookmarks can easily be constructed that outline important partner strategies and reminders. See Appendices A and B for bookmark ideas to get you started. Children love to have their personal strategy bookmarks laminated and placed in the "bookmark can" for all to borrow and enjoy. Strategy bookmarks might include:

   - ways to help my partner
   - what to do when reading is hard
   - how to choose just-right books
   - rules for partners
   - ways to talk about the story with my partner

5. *Reading phones.* When children read with partners, voice volume can be a problem. "Reading phones" made from PVC piping allow the reader to speak softly while still letting the listener hear clearly and enhancing his or her awareness of fluency. (Prescott-Griffin & Witherell 2004). These inexpensive "elbow pipes" can be found in any building supply store.

6. *Pointers and glasses.* Being able to use funny glasses and interesting pointers often enhances partners' enjoyment of and involvement in reading. Glasses and pointers are frequently used by children when "reading around the room," but they can also be useful for partners, particularly when they have chosen to share big books together.

7. *Reading pillows.* Reading pillows can be used to sit on or as a "reading desk." When partners read, if I notice that books are wobbling and wiggling to the detriment of smooth, thoughtful reading, I model the use of a "reading pillow," or lap desk. I then suggest that partners search together for a just-right pillow to use for this purpose.

■ Setting Up Successful Partnerships

When teachers implement peer partnerships, they make possible important connections to all aspects of the literacy program. These relationships afford readers time to practice and refine skills and strategies learned during read-aloud discussions, shared reading, and guided reading. In a peer partnership, children build fluency and comprehension while developing the collaborative relationships so important to literate classroom communities, relationships that blur the lines between school and home, mimicking the more social reading of parent and child at home. Some of the questions I ask myself when planning for successful peer partnerships are:

- What makes a compatible partner? What factors should I take into account when pairing children? Who should decide?

- When in the school year should peer partnerships begin and when do they fit in the school day?

- How do I help when partnerships are not working? Should I step in? How?

The Art of Pairing Students

First-grader Pete says, "My partner knows me . . . he really knows what books I like, and I know him. We can find books for each other and ourselves." First grade teacher Kristen Vito says, "There is an artistry in pairing, finding just the right partnership, coming up with the just-right pair who will accentuate one another's strengths and shore up weaknesses." I agree. Pairing is all about listening to children and getting to know their academic, social, and emotional needs. If we are to pair children compatibly, we must learn about their passions and interests, their likes and dislikes, their preferences and friendships. Sometimes friends make excellent partners; sometimes they don't. Often partnerships lead to friendships; sometimes they don't.

During writing workshop, I might pair stronger writers with those still struggling with the process. During math class, cross-ability pairing allows all children to be successful and participate fully during explorations and investigative activities. My first graders have fourth-grade reading buddies who help them do research and practice their reading. However, during peer partner reading, although many variations and pairings are possible, children should be paired with readers of *approximately equal expertise*. Equal expertise does not mean the same expertise, and each partner brings his or her individual strengths to the partnership. But with peer readers there is less chance of one partner usurping the task from the other, and more opportunity to put heads together and problem-solve text.

Pairing decisions vary according to the social, emotional, and cognitive needs of each classroom of readers. Because peer partnerships differ in form, purpose,

FIG. 3–4 *Partners thinking*

and structure from classroom to classroom, teachers make pairing decisions in many different ways. At times, teachers pair children spontaneously for a particular activity. Sharon Roberts says:

Sometimes I let them choose partners; sometimes it was, "You two, then you and you," according to where they were seated. Other times, I'd think about social things. Two girls were very motherly, very nurturing, and they worked really well with certain children. I didn't have them read over and over with the same person, because I wanted to give them choices.

What Pairing Looks Like in My Classroom

To be sure my partnerships include readers of approximately equal expertise, I make the pairing decisions. I also believe children need time to develop and structure collaborative reading relationships. Therefore, unless partners are experiencing difficulties, reading partners in my first-grade classroom remain together for six to eight weeks. During that time, pairs may join together in a larger partnership for a time or shift and change slightly, but by and large they remain together, building and strengthening their literate relationships. As Rosie says, "When we make a mistake, we know how to help each other. We just know how to do it. Like today, I made a little mistake and Elizabeth showed me. Reading with each other is important because you can read quicker and better." To support children's collaborations, I confer with partners, present minilessons, and introduce brainstorming sessions focused on strategies for reading collaboratively with one's partner.

What Pairing Looks Like in Other Classrooms

Some teachers allow readers to choose partners from members of their guided reading group. Others, like Kristen Vito, let students choose whether to partner-read at all. Although Kristen occasionally pairs children for reading or writing, for the most part she allows them to choose partners in accordance with "whatever passion is driving them at the time"—interests, friendships, ability. Occasionally Kristen also pairs children at different levels, encouraging a stronger reader to share an interest, ability, or passion with a weaker one.

Sharon Roberts' students occasionally choose their own partners, but usually Sharon assigns partners so that children "work with readers who are compatible in terms of ability as well as social and emotional needs." Anne Santoro allows her first graders to rechoose their partners every day, as long as they choose someone from their guided reading group.

Joy Richardson groups peers in several ways. First, she groups children for guided reading based on reading level and learning needs, and these groups then read independently in "buddy circles." Joy assists buddy circle members by providing tools like book bags to help readers organize and structure their interactions (see Chapter 7 for more on buddy circles). During center time, children choose a buddy from their center group. Because students usually go to centers with members of their guided reading group, they are able to partner with a reader at approximately the same level. When Joy asks peer partners to reread familiar stories for practice, she usually makes the grouping decisions, so that most readers are paired with someone of approximately equal expertise.

A Final Word About Pairing

No matter how teachers pair readers or for how long, they need to respect what students are telling them about what works and what does not. It is important to remember that partner reading is about relationships as well as reading the words and getting the meaning: "When I read with my buddy, it's like a brother. He knows me like a brother."

■ How Time Considerations Impact Partnerships

When to Begin Peer Partnerships

Although peer partnerships can be introduced at varying times during the school year, I begin mine on the first day of first grade. During the early weeks of school, I continue to encourage children to "partner up" during reading workshop. Early-in-the-year partnering helps children stay involved with books a little longer even when they are convinced that they "can't read." It also helps children become acquainted or reacquainted socially. In these early days before I have determined students' reading level, children are free to choose their own partner. If a child is at loose ends during reading workshop, I might suggest he read with someone, but usually children find each other. Once I have a sense of students' emotional, academic, and social needs, I pair children for partner reading. At less structured times and occasionally during reading workshop, students are still free to choose their own partners.

Some teachers begin partner reading as a center activity. They introduce and model the behavior they expect partners to use in the center and review these rules often. Rules are kept simple in the beginning and are usually posted in the center.

Still others, like Joy Richardson, begin the year using partnerships to practice rereading familiar stories and then, midyear, introduce buddy circles, in which children read independently in their already established guided reading groups. Joy says that by midyear her students have become comfortable working cooperatively and independently in small groups and buddy circles are thus more independent and productive than they would be earlier in the year.

How Often to Use Peer Partnerships

Whether to use peer partnerships daily or weekly depends on each class of students and their literacy needs. Some years I decide early on to implement small-group guided reading as the most conducive structure for developing readers. Other years, I move children toward independence almost immediately and let children partner-read or read alone much of every day.

Once peer partnerships are established, I generally ask children to partner-read first thing in the morning, three or four days a week, depending on the week's schedule. After children enter and complete their morning jobs, they find their partner, grab their books, and read for twenty or thirty minutes. I find partner reading, like journal writing, eases children's transition from home to school and sets a literate, focused tone for the day ahead. In addition to this established, early-morning time, I often allow readers to partner during reading workshop later in the morning.

Peer partner reading can take place at any number of times throughout the school day. Some teachers use partner reading as a transition between recess and a formal reading period. Others offer it as a choice during independent reading. You need to choose when and how often you use partner reading according to your own literacy program and group of children.

By February or March, as children move toward fluency, I begin to de-emphasize partnerships, leaving partnering as a choice, but not requiring that children read together. By this time, peer partnerships have done their job. They have brought children joyfully and collaboratively closer to reading independence.

■ What to Do When Partnerships Aren't Working

Anticipating challenges that may arise for partners enables you to provide timely support through conferences, intervention, and instruction. Despite my best efforts to support and encourage peer partners' collaborative behavior, there are times, especially in the start-up weeks, when partnerships experience friction and are less than productive.

In describing interactions of first-grade partners, MacGillivray (1997) writes that "children [show] their growing realization that it is prestigious to attend to exact print" (p. 145). My observations of struggling partners reveal that they are indeed well aware of the prestige involved in attending to and reading text exactly. Often, weaker skills and the accompanying feelings of diminished prestige when reading with others leads to negative behavior during partner reading, such as hiding the book or making angry faces or comments. At other times, partners revert to less mature kinds of reading, such as reading the pictures or pretending to read. Often the readers who experience problems are not the weakest readers in the class, but for one reason or other they possess less confidence and perceive themselves as less able than their peers.

In the beginning, when I observe negative partner behavior, I sit with a partnership, highlighting positive behavior when it occurs and redirecting interactions when they take a negative turn. If such interventions do not succeed in changing the tone of a partnership, I switch the pairing or suggest that the struggling partnership work temporarily with another, more successful partnership. In facilitating this process, I'll then spend several days with a foursome, guiding their reading and interactions. (See Chapter 9 for additional suggestions and strategies for supporting struggling partnerships as well as ideas for assisting collaboration once partnerships are well established.)

Beginning Lessons for Effective Peer Partnerships

4

S haron Roberts gathers her class for a midmorning shared reading of *Citybook* (Rotner & Kresiler 1996). Before beginning, Sharon tells the children that "the words in this book are tough, but if you look at the pictures, you'll be able to figure them out." Sharon leads a choral reading of the text, then begins a short discussion focusing on the story's sequence. As children share, she jots vocabulary and events on chart paper in the order in which they happened in the story. Later, when children pair for reading, Sharon asks them to replicate what they've just done—read the story, using the pictures to help; retell the story; and make notes in the correct sequence.

Teachers continually provide students with minilessons on and models of effective reading. Fosnot (1996) argues that strategy lessons and explicit modeling "perturb" learners, contradicting what they think is good reading behavior. After these experiences, children return to reading with new, evaluative perspectives with which to examine their own behavior. Calkins (2001) provides what she calls an "architecture of a minilesson" (p. 84) that can help you plan and teach effective, relevant minilessons. Calkins' five components are:

1. Begin the lesson by making a *connection* to material currently under study.
2. *Teach* the new skill or strategy.
3. Provide opportunities for students to be *actively involved* in the lesson.
4. *Link* the lesson to readers' lives and current literacy work.

5. Bring the group back together after individuals practice independently and *follow up.* (pp. 84–85)

Whether reading aloud, presenting book talks, or conducting focused, explicit minilessons about reading processes, procedures, and skills, teachers provide children with the models and structures necessary to be successful (see Appendix C for ideas and suggestions for general reading minilessons). Teaching is ongoing throughout the school year, planned and executed to respond to readers' needs at a given moment. Along with these daily instructional activities, teachers who use peer partnerships regularly present or facilitate lessons and discussions centering around expectations for partnerships and partner behavior.

These teachers also conduct a number of minilessons specifically focused on strategies for partner reading. For example, first-grade teacher Anne Santoro models and discusses different ways to take turns—alternate pages; read chorally; each read a book, then switch—then allows her students to select the turn-taking structure that best suits the text they are reading and the needs of the partnership. Anne also leads students in discussions about the strategies partners should keep in mind. These strategies include "look for a chunk you know," skip over and read for meaning, use the pictures, and "help your partner start the word."

Anne expects her students to work responsibly and collaboratively during partner reading. Her directions are clear and explicit, and she conveys her trust in her students' ability to meet and exceed her expectations. Their actions reflect these expectations. As David says, "I help my partner out a little bit. If I missed a word, he would tell me. It's important that you listen to your buddy." Students' understanding of what it means to be a good partner is evident in their partner interactions and in the ways they describe their work during these times: "My partner helps me with words I don't know. He might say 'animal' if it was a horse, and when I find a chunk in there, I can tell him. I find the first letter, then the chunk."

When planning lessons that support peer partnerships and students' collaborations, it is important to ask such questions as:

- What types of modeling and demonstrations will support effective peer partnerships?

- What kinds of charts and rules should be created to assist partners and remind them about strategies?

- How do we help peer partners make good book choices?

Each teacher voices expectations for partner reading slightly differently, although the underlying messages are the same:

- Be supportive.

- Collaborate.

- Stay on task.

"I expect both partners to be reading the same book. That's a given," says Christine Wiltshire. "And they should help if their partner gets stuck. Do what the teacher would do. In other words, hint, don't tell. Look at the first letter, maybe tell the first letter." Later, when I interviewed Christine's students, they articulated these same ideas—"Do what the teacher would do" and "Tell the first sound or letter"—indicating that they had internalized the messages of Christine's direct and persuasive teaching.

"We model, model, model, then we model some more," says Kristen Vito, explaining how she and her student teacher provide demonstrations on all facets of reading and writing processes, procedures, and skills. When I visited midyear, Kristen told me that she had been stressing the importance of punctuation in making meaning and that she now "noticed them coaching one another on how to use punctuation to read effectively." As with Christine's students, Kristen's modeling was reflected in the children's partner reading behavior and in the ways they talked about reading process during interviews with me. Anna said, "If you don't know a word, reading can be really hard. Usually people read an excitement mark [exclamation points], but some people don't read it. I didn't read it, but my partner pointed and helped me read it, you know, with excitement."

■ Teaching Ideas

All teachers expect that partners will remain on task and engaged when reading together. In addition to this overall expectation, teachers often have specific ideas about how partnerships should work. If we listen, children also tell us *what they need to know* in order to be effective readers and collaborators. The ideas for teaching and modeling outlined below come from the teachers and students I have observed using peer partnerships. The list is by no means inclusive, but merely a starting point for thinking about strategies for reading partnerships:

1. *Partner positions.* Model and discuss the importance of sitting side by side. Occasionally I will find a teacher who uses back-to-back or ear-to-ear positions, but for most readers, sharing a book side by side works best.

FIG. 4–1

2. *Voice and volume.* Discuss the importance of quiet voices. Most readers prefer quiet when they read. In a room of twenty first graders, all reading aloud, this may be hard to achieve. We want our classrooms to hum with industry during partner reading, not echo with the cacophony of many raised voices. Some suggestions for helping readers attend to voice and volume are:

- Use "five-inch voices."
- Use "inside voices."
- Use "whispering voices."
- Use "reading phones" made with plastic tubing.

Making children aware of the importance of modulating voice volume allows all partners to focus on their reading with minimal distraction. My favorite description of appropriate partner reading voice level is Justin's: "When I read with buddies, I gotta find the lowest voice in my body."

3. *Taking turns.* With a student volunteer, model different ways to take turns:

- Read chorally, or "both together."
- Alternate pages.
- Alternate two or three pages. (For fiction, especially, I find it helps the flow of the story to encourage children to read several pages before switching. For younger readers, this is sometimes more difficult than

alternating single pages, but it can be introduced once partnerships are well established.)

4. *Hinting rather than telling.* With a student volunteer, rehearse and demonstrate how to "hint rather than tell" when one's partner struggles with an unknown word.

5. *How reading should sound and look.* This is always fun! When reading a big book or chart story, I pause every so often to talk about "how it sounds," asking students to critique my reading. I might direct their attention to pacing, expression, the importance of attending to punctuation, or text anomalies such as bold or italicized text.

6. *Debriefing after reading.* Debriefing allows time to highlight successes and provide explicit teaching. At the close of partner reading, bring students together and ask partners what worked and what they might do differently next time. (I also highlight behavior and strategies partners might try based on my observations of the day's interactions.)

7. *Word solving as meaning making.* Pay attention to the experiences children bring to school and the developmental nature of first graders' evolving repertoire of word-solving strategies. As Sharon Roberts says, "Telling your partner 'look at the picture,' that's their best strategy at the beginning of the year. As the year moves on, I want them to think about the story and about word and letter patterns—consonant blends, vowel patterns. I want them to think more about what makes sense in certain contexts, and about words and word parts. As the year goes on, yes, the picture might help, but the more difficult the book, the less picture support there is. So I tend to move them away from the illustrations as their word solving gets stronger. I want them really to look at the word, because chances are they know something about it and they can help their partner."

8. *When to help and when to hold back.* Some children tend to usurp the task at the first sign their partner is struggling. Reinforce the importance of waiting for partners to "have a go" or ask for help before stepping in. When a partner does ask for help, some teachers want the listener to hint, give a clue, or provide a scaffold, not take complete control of the reading. Other teachers believe that maintaining fluent meaning is more important. In that case, "telling the word" or "reading a little bit together" are more expedient strategies than hinting or giving a clue. Whatever our preference, we need to appreciate that students may not necessarily define reading with a partner

as we do. Despite our coaching and modeling, young readers are often reluctant to break the flow of story, reluctant to pause in their mutually defined meaning making to hint and provide wait time. This emphasis on fluency and meaning when reading with a partner should be respected and applauded, for it reveals children's deep understanding of the purpose and process of reading.

■ Strategy Charts

Once partnerships are established, it is helpful to discuss and share strategies as a class. I hold such meetings at least once a week, and while I facilitate the discussions, most often they become brainstorming sessions in which I solicit the children's ideas, write their responses on chart paper, and post it on the wall. By early October, my students are experienced "brainstormers"—their ideas and suggestions have already been solicited to establish class and playground rules, plan science and social study units, and select projects for the twice weekly afternoon "activity time" (arts and crafts, holiday-related events, science and art museum field trips, and so on).

Creating and posting peer partnership strategy charts that can be added to throughout the year provide visual reminders to children about responsible collaborative behavior. If we want students to make use of these tools, the ideas and suggestions must come from them. As the charts grow, the ideas written on them reflect growth in children's literate thinking. A simple early list might be:

1. Use quiet reading voices.
2. Let both partners read.
3. Follow along when your partner is reading.
4. Help your partner when he or she needs it.

As the year progresses and children's understanding of expectations grows, the chart can be extended. For example "help your partner" might have sub-entries like:

- Say, "Try to sound it out."

- Say, "Find a little word in the big word."

- Ask, "What can I do to help you?"

- Ask, "What would make sense?"

- Say, "Look at the pictures."

FIG. 4–2 *Chart of "How to help my partner"*

- Say, "The first sound is [make the sound of the first letter]."

- Say, "It rhymes with [rhyming word]."

- Give a hint. For example, if the word is *horse,* say, "It's a kind of animal."

If all children are to have access to the literate understanding of their classmates, setting aside time to discuss, share, and record ideas is critical. Reviewing these charts reminds readers of these important strategies. Children continually amaze me with their understanding of the reading process and their child-centered strategies for supporting and helping each other:

- "The word begins like my name."

- "Remember, we sang a song about that."

- "Why don't you use your finger?"

- "Try reading it one more time, a little slower."

- "Look at that mark [exclamation point]. It means excitement!"

- "Those black letters mean you read loud!"

- "Remember, you read that word up here."

- "Let's sing it, like the tune."

- "I'll make a frame [using fingers] so you can see the word better."

Sharon Roberts prefers to wait until peer partners have worked together a while before creating strategy charts, so that ideas flow more easily:

Making a partner strategy chart wasn't this big, labored "let's make another chart" thing. After they got rolling, it was just a matter of "What are the things we need to remember when we're partner reading?" We often go back to "What are you going to do if your partner gets stuck on a word?" And all that language comes out again, strategies and what not. The essential part in the beginning for me is "What does this look like and what does it sound like?" That's how we started the year. I didn't bring in the "criteria for success chart" until about two months into school, maybe around November. This was purposeful: they had to know themselves "what works and what doesn't when I'm partner reading" so they were able to generate a list. If it were my list, it would be meaningless.

No matter when we decide to create charts, if we want children to use them, we must create charts *with them*. Possibilities for charts are endless, but here are a few ideas:

- Rules for partners.

- What can I do to help my partner?

- What can I do when my partner doesn't know a word?

- Thinking strategies partners use.

Rules for Partnerships

Teachers who implement peer partner reading usually work with students to create "rules for partner reading." These might be stated and reviewed at the start of each partner reading session, or they might be listed on a chart or

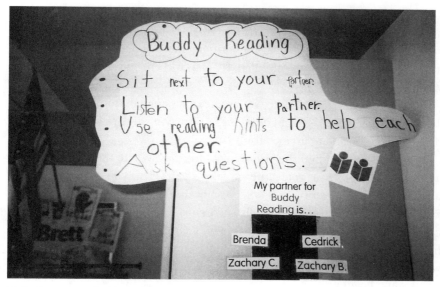

FIG. 4–3 *Anne's buddy reading rules chart*

blackboard. Wherever they are posted, rules evolve and grow as peer partnerships evolve and grow. Many teachers begin by specifying rules about taking turns, but then, as Kristen Vito recommends, "Let the children negotiate what works best for them." Some partners work better alternating pages; others prefer choral reading. Some books lend themselves to choral reading, while others are more fun to read taking turns. Once partners have experienced and practiced many structures, they should and can be trusted to choose what works best, provided they stay on task.

Early in the year, during interactive writing, Anne Santoro and her students create a chart listing ideas for buddy reading (see photograph). This chart is then prominently displayed in the circle area, and Anne often refers to it at the start of buddy reading, thereby reinforcing these rules and routines.

■ Helping Partners Make Appropriate Book Choices

Early one January day, Joy Richardson gathers her students on the carpet to preview books they may choose later in the day for reading workshop and partner reading. Most of these new books are in browsing boxes marked with the levels F–J (based on the criteria in Fountas and Pinnell 1996). Joy holds up each title and gives a mini–book talk, often making a connection to another story they have read or suggesting ways they might read the book alone or with buddies.

One of Joy's recommendations is *Chicken Little* (Giles 1997), written in script form. "Remember when we read *Henny Penny?* (Zimmerman 1989) This is another version of that story. What do you remember about *Henny Penny?*" Paul says, "It had a duck." Deidre chimes in, "And a chicken, and she thought the sky was falling."

Joy says, "You're right. There were some other animals, too, weren't there?" She flips through the pages of *Chicken Little,* displaying illustrations. Jessica contributes, "A goose and a turkey, I think."

Joy shows the children the beginning of the play, where there is a chart listing each character. "See, you can each take a part. First, you and your partner can read through the story, so it will be smooth, then you can each take a part and act out the story." She then tells children she has placed a number of play scripts in the browsing boxes, each based on a familiar fairy or folktale. She also shows them where they can find five more copies of each script in case they want to read in their buddy circle. Following Joy's book talk, students take out journals and begin writing.

If we show interest and enthusiasm for books, children will too. Joy's quick minilesson sets the stage for students' book selection later in the morning, piquing readers' interest and generating excitement for what lies ahead. Her students carry many ideas away from Joy's book talk on how to use books alone or with buddies. Planning is important for readers and writers, and Joy gives first graders plenty of planning time. As students write, enjoy their snack break, and participate in morning circle, they anticipate and organize their thinking about reading tasks ahead. Then, when it is time for buddy reading, they are prepared and ready. Instead of spending the first ten minutes wandering around in search of books, students make selections quickly and spend the majority of reading time reading.

Many times, I hear teachers voice frustration about students who spend the entire reading workshop browsing for books. Reluctant readers are especially good at browsing. Even though I believe that browsing is a wonderfully literate activity, underrated in our busy world, I want my students to spend partner and solo reading sessions reading. Having appropriate just-right books in their hands at the start enables reading to happen, thus affording young readers the practice and problem solving they need to become confident, fluent, thoughtful readers.

As Joy's book talk illustrates, an important part of readers workshop is highlighting wonderful literature for children and suggesting books and reading materials they might like. As teachers, we must model and demonstrate for children how to make good, appropriate book choices and have good book-related discussions. We can also ask students to model and demonstrate for their peers how they select just-right books.

I want students to pursue their passions and interests, even in books that may not be at their reading level. Therefore my students are free to choose widely, regardless of level, for solo and partner reading. I do, however, specify that "most" of their selections be just-right books. That way I can be sure that the majority of their time will be spent reading at a comfortable level. Most children respect this "rule"; only occasionally do I have to remind children about making good reading choices during partner reading.

Appropriate book selection is something I emphasize in many instructional contexts, from reading aloud to shared and guided reading. Initially, children may need more structure—fewer choices and more teacher direction; however, as the year goes on, I want to respect their choices and provide organizational structures that enhance the time they spend reading. As Cheryl Feeney says, "Book handling, we spend a lot of time with that. We get them really familiar with how to choose books wisely, how to handle and take care of them. Then we give them a book basket, later replaced with book baggies. These baggies have common books in them, so that partners will have the same titles."

Cheryl and her teaching partner, Jo-Ann Gettings, ask children to reread familiar or "common" books from their baggies during partner reading. These may be big books they have read together during shared reading or texts they have read and practiced during guided reading. Partners may also reread previously practiced stories from a school's reading anthology, concentrating on fluency.

Through teacher introductions of read-aloud books and shared reading texts as well as their experiences during guided reading, partners learn how to introduce themselves to books—how to open, skim, preview, and decide whether they want to read more.

Teachers like Kristen Vito stress daily the importance of making "good choices." For Kristen, good choices might be just-right books at children's independent reading level or "more difficult books that they are motivated to try," like Rylant's Henry and Mudge series:

> There are times when I make a conscious effort to steer children to a more difficult book than they can really read, if they have the will. Like with Henry and Mudge. They all love Mudge and want to read those books. They might not actually be able to yet, but pairing them with a buddy helps gives them access, and that's really powerful for me. This can really give struggling readers an adrenalin shot when they need it—they can do it and feel empowered. Partner reading gives them access to texts that maybe otherwise they would not have access to.

Giving children access to texts is important for both solo and tandem readers. Whether we are talking up great books, helping children select just-right books, or celebrating their efforts to construct more challenging text with partners, we provide young readers with access to a wide variety of texts as they build the skills they will need to lead literate lives in and out of school.

■ Summing Up

In your beginning lessons for partners, you should:

- Introduce and model strategies through your own and student demonstrations.

- Allow group time in which children can share and discuss strategies that work and rules for effective partnering.

- Listen and observe what is happening in partnerships with an eye toward planning future modeling and instruction.

- Trust readers to make good choices, selecting strategies and structures that work for them.

As a busy teacher always looking for new strategies, I especially appreciate lists of ideas for quick minilessons. Appendix D summarizes the partner reading strategies outlined in this chapter, as well as many others. To be most effective, these minilessons should be modeled both by you and by students in your class. The list provided is just a beginning; as always, you should develop lessons based on the needs, interests, and learning preferences of your students.

Taking Turns and Leading

5

We open our books, then look at the pictures. Then we go back and read.
We just get books, someone picks one, and we read.
We ask who wants to go first, then we read.
Put 'em in a pile. Take turns. Read.

As I watch children's interactions and talk with them about how they read together, I am struck by the structures and routines partners develop to help relationships run smoothly. Sometimes their activities resemble or mimic the structures and procedures of guided reading or shared reading. At other times the routines they adopt are their own and bear little relation to routines or structures teachers have suggested or recommended.

In thinking about taking turns and being the leader in peer partnerships, it is important to ask:

- What turn-taking procedures seem to promote and enhance collaboration?

- What types of turn-taking procedures do I need to teach and model for readers?

- What effective turn-taking and organizational strategies do I observe partners using that should be shared with the whole class?

- What kinds of specific organizational strategies do partnerships need to be effective?

■ Taking Turns

"We find where we want to sit. Then we see who wants to go first. I let him go first."

"Well, today I felt like reading last. I was out sick yesterday."

"I let him go first, and sometimes he lets me go first."

"We do rock–paper–scissors shoot, and whoever wins goes first."

Turn-taking decisions vary with the kind of text selected, text difficulty, teacher instructions, and partner preferences. Sometimes readers begin a book taking turns one way, then switch to another that better suits the text and the readers' needs. Often partners discuss or negotiate turn taking as they move from one text to the next. The following interaction occurs as Nancy and Freddie complete Freddie's book, reading every other page, and prepare to read Nancy's choice, *Henry and Mudge Get the Cold Shivers* (Rylant 1997).

Nancy	**Freddie**
[Holds up the book] Now, we go to this one—*Henry and Mudge Get the Cold Shivers*. [Moves closer to Freddie and turns to the title page]	
	Henry and Mudge Get the Cold Shivers.
[Turns to the table of contents]	
	[Points] *A big* . . . [pauses on the word *kiss*]
Okay, I'm going to read one and a half pages. I mean, one and a half chapters.	
	What about me?
Okay, you read the other half.	
	[Points] That last one?
[Flips to page 5] Okay, we're gonna do one page at a time, okay?	
	[Lies down] We're not gonna do the whole book. Only one chapter.
No, we're gonna do all of it.	
	Why? That's too much!
[Shrugs and begins reading]	

As it happens, Freddie is saved by the bell: partner reading ends just as they complete reading Chapter 1. In their next partner reading session, Nancy again insists they read a chapter of *Henry and Mudge Get the Cold Shivers.* At the chapter's conclusion, however, Freddie's wishes prevail and they switch to a book of his choosing.

Although all conversations about turn taking are not as one-sided as the example above, they usually involve a suggestion on the part of one reader followed by a brief discussion, after which the partners usually immediately begin reading. Experienced partners usually make these decisions with alacrity, eager to get started. For example, Bobby holds up a copy of *Ira Sleeps Over* (Waber 1972) and says, "We have to read this first." His partner Pete replies, "Read, mister! You go first."

Conversations about turn taking may occur before, during, or after reading as partners make decisions about tasks ahead. For example, Patrick and Eddie complete their reading and prepare to retell the story. Patrick says, "I'll talk about the beginning, you talk about the middle, I'll talk about the end. Okay?" Eddie nods. "Okay!"

Truly fluent reading involves continual attention to understanding. Fluent readers ask questions as they move purposefully through text. Fluent readers convey the author's meaning through engaged, interpretive reading of the text. No matter what turn-taking routines I suggest or encourage, my focus is always on helping partners read with understanding. If the turn-taking structure partners are using does not support meaningful reading, I step in to suggest and model alternatives. Typically, peer partners take turns in one of these six ways:

- They alternate reading one, two, or three pages.

- They alternate reading sentences.

- They read chorally.

- One reader echoes the other.

- They each assume the roles of different characters in the story.

- One reader reads an entire book, then the other reader reads an entire book.

Reading Alternate Pages

"We each read a side of the book."

"It's all about sharing. What you have to do is just let one person have a turn reading a page or two or three, then the next person reads. And that's how you do it!"

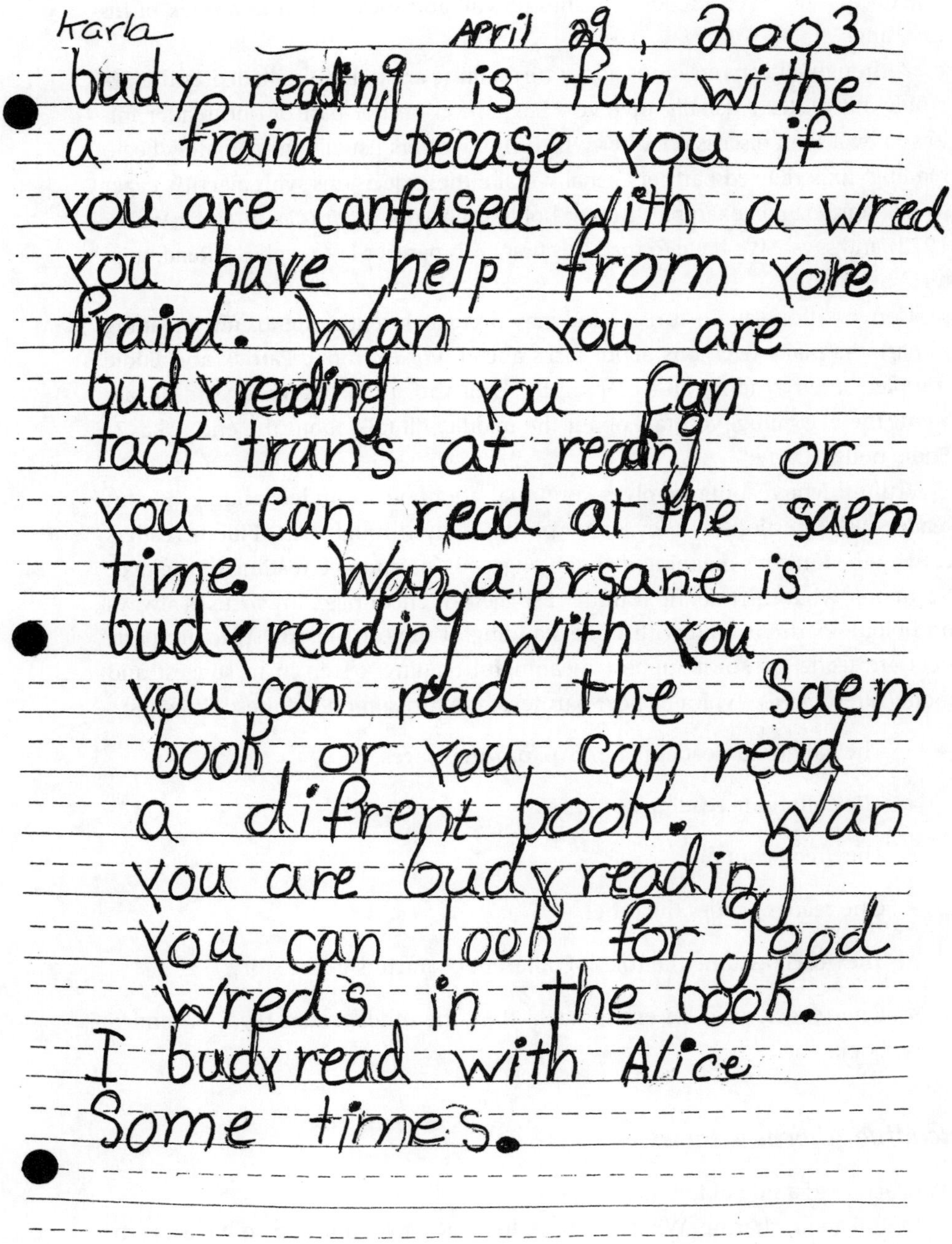

Karla   April 29, 2003
• budy reading is fun withe
a fraind becase you if
you are canfused with a wred
you have help from yore
fraind. Wan you are
budy reading you can
tack trans at reading or
you can read at the saem
time. Wan a prsane is
• budy reading with you
you can read the saem
book or you can read
a difrent book. Wan
you are budy reading
you can look for good
wreds in the book.
I budy read with Alice
Some times.
•

FIG. 5–1 *Student writing about turn taking*

Alternating pages, or "each reading a side of the book," is one way we encourage children to read as partners. This turn-taking structure allows partners to assume the role of both reader and listener/assistant during the reading of every book. While the reader reads her page, the listener's job is to follow along, offering assistance or support as needed.

For younger readers, alternating every other page is probably easiest. As children move into texts with more complex stories and more than a few words on each page, however, I encourage them to alternate after two or three pages so that partners get caught up in the story before switching. From the first day of school, I talk with children about the most important part of reading—thinking and making sense. One of the major reasons I ask students to "partner up" is to keep the focus on meaning and fluency. It is often a delicate balancing act, keeping both partners equally engaged and meaning intact while reading larger and larger "chunks" of text; however, it is a worthwhile goal as we move readers toward fluency and deeper understanding.

Alternating Sentence by Sentence

"He usually reads a sentence, then I read a sentence."

Occasionally, teachers ask partners to read every other sentence, usually to ensure that both readers stay on task. Sometimes children adopt this sentence-by-sentence turn taking on their own. Although I do not intervene without first listening to how things are going, I do not encourage sentence-by-sentence or paragraph-by-paragraph reading; in most cases it interrupts the flow of story and meaning is lost.

Choral Reading

"I read the title of the book. We don't take turns. We just go reading and reading and reading until the book is finished."

Many partners choose "reading and reading and reading until the book is finished," because it allows both readers (or a larger group in the case of buddy circles) to read the whole text. Much like guided reading, choral reading allows readers to experience the text in its entirety instead of stopping and starting. For most of us, the joy of reading is becoming swept up in story or topic, losing ourselves in the vicarious pleasure of the journey through text. We should respect young readers' desire to do the same, allowing them the choice to "read and read" when they feel it's appropriate. Some texts particularly suited for choral reading are:

- poems

- picture books incorporating the text of familiar songs, such as *Wheels on the Bus* (Wickstrom 1985) or *Seals on the Bus* (Hart 2000)

- rhyming, rhythmic texts

Echo Reading

"I have a go, then she repeats, and we do that till it's over."

When parents ask how they can help their child with reading, my first suggestion is to read all kinds of text aloud. My second suggestion is usually echo reading. My first graders echo-read with their fourth-grade partners, the more experienced fourth grader going first, the first grader echoing. Typically, the first reader reads a small chunk of text—a page, a paragraph, or a few clearly marked lines—and pauses at a logical break. Then the second reader "echoes" what's been read. Echo reading in cross-ability pairs enables the less experienced reader to experience fluent reading of text slightly above his reading level and exposes him to more complex vocabulary, sentence structures, and language patterns.

With modeling and support, echo reading can also be a beneficial and supportive way for peer partners to share reading. When I talk about echo reading with young readers, I say that the first reader "plows the way" and the second reader "sows the seeds." I tell them that the first reading may be bumpy, with rocks and roots to slow the plow's way. After the plow does its work, however, the seeder can make things smooth, reading with pacing and expression. Because the first reader's job is so much more difficult, I usually encourage children to switch roles *often*.

Mine isn't a perfect metaphor, but it helps me explain the two roles and helps children appreciate that the first reader's role is much harder. This helps partners "plow" into echo reading with a collaborative, pioneering spirit.

Taking Character Parts

"Squawk, squawk, squawk! I'll be the chick, you be the duckling, then we'll switch!"

Children love to take the parts of characters in stories. As they assume roles and act out the story, they practice and refine parts of the text that they can then read with fluency and expression. There are many books that lend themselves to this type of turn taking, and I am always on the lookout for more.

Read an Entire Book, Then Switch

"I read my favorite book, then she reads hers."

Of all turn-taking structures, reading whole texts to each other is the one I see used least often, perhaps because teachers do not encourage this type of structure. Although it can work, it is sometimes difficult for the listening partner to pay attention through the reading of an entire text in which she takes no active part. If readers want to use this structure, I encourage them to read shorter books or pause several times during the reading to talk about the story. Specifically, I suggest they:

- Choose a book that's "short and lively."

- Choose books together, no matter who will read each one.

- Sit close together.

- Assign the listener a job, such as turning pages or pointing to where to begin on each page.

- Talk about the title and take a "picture walk" through the book before beginning to read it.

- Stop halfway through and ask a question.

- If the book is short, let the listener reread it with lots of expression.

- Switch to another type of turn taking after each reader has read one whole book.

Most of these suggestions are things that help the listener pay attention. Partners who use this strategy often come up with their own attention-keeping strategies. For example, when Bobby reads the short patterned text *Along Comes Jake* (Cowley 1987), he notices that Pete's attention is wandering. To call his partner back, Bobby devises an amusing innovation: instead of reading the repeating chorus "And then along comes Jake!" Bobby reads "And then along comes Jack-Jake!" The name *Jack* does not appear in the text but is Bobby's alliterative invention. Each time Bobby says *Jack-Jake*, Pete refocuses, laughing, smiling, or giving him a nudge. Bobby's strategy ensures that his audience stays with him.

Partners' Positions

"I read a page, then I turn it and he reads, and we turn it and turn it and turn it."

"I read, then pass the book, then she'll read and pass to me."

The children above are describing how they read alternating pages when the partners sit catty-corner to each other. However, I encourage children to sit side by side so that both readers have equal access to text. I also encourage listeners to offer both verbal and nonverbal kinds of assistance. This is easier to do when sitting shoulder to shoulder.

Teachers' Thoughts About Turn Taking

Sharon Roberts says, "Initially, I provide a lot of structure. I say, 'These are the two ways you can read this piece—go every other page or read it together.' I give them different ways to break up a book so they can be successful reading it together. I find this is essential in the beginning. Later I phase this out." Like Sharon, many teachers specify that peer partners use certain structures or turn-taking routines early on, believing that this initial structuring will help children establish collaborative relationships more quickly and easily. In specifying routines, we give partners a chance to practice many ways to read before choosing the ways that suit them best.

Like Sharon, Jenny Baumeister models several turn-taking structures—choral reading, alternating pages, reading whole books to each other—so that children become familiar with a variety of strategies. Usually she then asks partners to try the structure she has just modeled. After readers have practiced all the ways of taking turns, Jenny steps back and lets partners decide which ones work best for them.

Teachers like Kristen Vito have "done it all." Whereas years earlier Kristen was quite specific about partner behavior, she now lets the relationships evolve:

I think so much of life is about communication and negotiating effectively. This is a really good skill for them to be working toward. They know that one child cannot read the entire text, but I let them negotiate that. I think they're so driven and they want to do it so much that they figure out the most comfortable way to do it. I trust the children to decide and negotiate what works best for them.

Most of the peer partners in Kristen's classroom choose to take turns by reading chorally. However, this type of turn taking is not without its challenges. When I queried her students about what they found difficult in reading chorally with a partner, they often mentioned that it was hard to stay together: "When they're reading, you might get mixed up. Sometimes they read, and they're on a different word than you. Like Jane was done with the whole page and I wasn't. Sometimes I read faster than her—sometimes I like reading slow."

Who goes first is something I trust partners to decide. Children are usually quite adept at determining who will read first, alternating this privilege fairly either book by book or day by day. I intervene only if the decision seems repeatedly lopsided or unfair. Likewise, I intervene when partners choose books only if an overbearing partner almost never allows his or her companion to have a say.

I usually model or ask students to model all kinds of turn-taking structures, then step away and observe, allowing partners to choose the ones that work best for them. When I observe partnerships, I always look for examples of effective turn taking, so that I can invite skillful collaborators to demonstrate how they read and share books for the class.

■ Being the Leader

"I start. Sometimes I go first, sometimes she does."

"I was the last to pick the book, so I go first tomorrow."

"If a person chooses a book, that person gets to go first. We take turns."

A successful partnership almost always requires a clearly defined leader. The leadership provided can be quiet and subtle or strong and overbearing; in most cases it positions somewhere in between. Once a leader is designated, the other partner (or partners in the case of "buddy circles"—see Chapter 7) respects and follows that lead, enabling the pair to stay on task.

In the interview excerpt below, it is clear that Nancy enjoys leading and possesses a keen sense of responsibility for the task and for the welfare of her peers:

Mary Lee: Who would you pick as your partner if you could choose anyone in the class?

Nancy: Well, I would pick somebody who I hadn't read with at all.

Mary Lee: Really? Why is that?

Nancy: Well, it would really be fairer to all the other kids.

Mary Lee: Fairer to the other kids? Tell me a little about that.

Nancy: Well, if I chose just one person and stuck with them, then all the other kids would feel very unhappy that I couldn't help them and read with them, so I would choose somebody who I hadn't read with.

In most of her partner interactions, Nancy perceives herself as the leader and takes her role very seriously. Like most effective leaders, she keeps the reading on track, taking the major responsibility for organizing procedures and negotiating a given text.

Ideally, children in peer reading partnerships share the leadership role, regularly switching who directs the way things go. The leadership role may switch with each book, or one child may act as leader for an entire partner session. I have even observed established partnerships in which one partner remains the leader for an entire week before switching.

Occasionally, there are children who always insist on leading, always want go first, always want to choose the books. Sometimes their partners allow them to, sometimes they don't. When I notice an unbalanced partnership, I suggest that the recessive partner be the leader for a particular session or that the pair choose who will lead and formally announce it before reading begins. Again, it is important to listen first, then intervene as needed to support fairer collaboration.

If a number of partners are experiencing friction around the issue of leadership, I lead a whole-class discussion about this topic, asking children to share how they decide who will lead or direct. Their answers are often surprising. They reveal not only children's ingenuity but also the many aspects of classroom life to which we, as teachers, are not always privy.

For example, Rosie says, "Well, the three of us sit at our little three-chair table. Then the leader of the group chooses the book and who reads. There's a different captain or leader every day. Yesterday, I was leader, today, Elizabeth, tomorrow, Cathy. It goes just like that."

When I tell Joy Richardson, Rosie's teacher, about the leadership structures Rosie's group has devised, Joy is surprised. This is the first she has heard of captains and leaders; she had no idea that these partners switched roles daily, in such a careful, ordered fashion.

■ Letting Children Figure It Out

"First, there's the title, and we read it. Then, we say 'once upon a time,' or we read the illustrator, or look at the pictures. Then we start reading."

If their confidence remains intact, primary-grade students are usually highly motivated, knowing that this is the year they will learn to read. If we give them the space, time, and encouragement as well as a compatible peer partner at their side, children usually figure out what to do about taking turns and being the leader.

My research suggests that when readers take turns reading every other page, they provide greater assistance and scaffolding to each other and engage in collaborative behavior more often at other times during the school day. Choral readers are also highly collaborative, their expertise shifting continuously as they construct text together, often word by word or phrase by phrase.

When readers take turns reading an entire book to each other, however, they are often not as engaged with each other and there is little collaboration. There are of course exceptions—some whole-book readers are very engaged and offer continual support and assistance to each other—but by and large it seems to be easier for children to share reading when they alternate pages or choral read.

Just as readers deserve choice and autonomy in where to sit, they also deserve the freedom to select the structures and organizational frameworks most appropriate for the text and the partnership. Although I model many ways to take turns, perhaps emphasizing that alternating pages is a collaborative way to read, if children want to "go reading and reading until the book is finished," I, and most of the teachers I have worked with, let partners choose, let them experiment, let them discover what works best for them.

6 | Listening to What Children Tell Us About Collaboration

Teaching is truly listening to children. Students humble me every day in teaching me how much more they are capable of, how much more than I ever dreamed.

—Kristen Vito, first-grade teacher

Each child, in every classroom, has her or his own unique learning preferences. Despite the accepted and perhaps necessary practice of warehousing students in schools in which they are often taught and expected to learn by the same methods and teaching approaches, learning remains a highly personal endeavor. When we listen, children tell us, through their actions and words, how they *prefer* to learn and grow.

During strategy discussions—and with little or no prompting on my part—children's ideas about "how to help my partner" draw on all-important aspects of the reading process while expressing the ways they prefer to learn. Even when their ideas reflect my teaching, students' wording is often more child-centered and peer-friendly than mine would be. Their ideas reveal a deep understanding and internalization of critical literacy concepts and an astute, insider's awareness of how best to assist and scaffold one another. The conversations, organizational decisions, modeling, and teaching that children engage in when they read together help me refine my thinking about peer partnerships.

▪ Defining Reading in Partnership

Cathy and Elizabeth sit side by side at a small table, each holding a copy of *The Carnival* (Hunt & Brychta 1997). They are on page 3:

Cathy	**Elizabeth**
They put it on a . . . [pauses on *trailer*]	
	[Points] *trailer.*
trailer. I get mixed up sometimes.	
[They turn to page 4]	
The children and dad . . . dress [for *dressed*] *up.*	
	[Points] *dressed*
dressed up.	

Elizabeth and Cathy are very involved and interested in this book. When Cathy pauses, unsure of the unfamiliar two-syllable word *trailer*, Elizabeth's eyes move back and forth from text to illustration. Once she has the "aha" and realizes the word is *trailer*, she blurts it out, forgetting her teacher's instructions about stopping and hinting. Which is more important—maintaining the flow of the story or stopping to hint and assist? Should teachers impose "rules" about hinting rather than telling the word? Gradual hinting may be appropriate in paired reading interactions in which an adult or more experienced reader actively scaffolds the process. But when children read with partners of approximately equal expertise, gradual hinting may be a hindrance to fluent meaning making.

Even though successful collaborators articulate, even internalize, the importance of hinting, they are often quick to step in when their partner struggles rather than go through the process of gradual hinting suggested by the teacher. My research reveals the most frequent cue peer partners employ is "telling the whole word" (Griffin 2000). This cue is also the most expedient, suggesting that the process of gradual hinting is too slow for peer partners reluctant to pause in their mutually defined process of making meaning.

After visiting and observing in dozens of classrooms I have discovered that teachers' intentions, purposes, and expectations for reading in partnership are often quite different from those of students. Whereas most teachers (I among them) view peer partner reading as a process in which the listening partner provides assistance as needed while ensuring that the reader retains ownership of the task, this may not be entirely appropriate. Although teachers' goals for partner assistance often center on *instruction* and the building and strengthening of the *individual* reader's skills, young readers' goals may, instead, focus on success for the *partnership*. Most often students that I have observed define success as smooth, fluent reading. Partners have a clear sense of the steps and procedures necessary to read successfully, and they demonstrate this understanding through their words and actions: "We read one page, then the other person reads the other page. Sometimes we read two pages. When people get stuck, we help them—help them sound it out."

Teachers are, of course, critical "partners in thought" and should never abdicate their teaching role, but I believe it is important sometimes to step back and acknowledge that children know better than we do what works best in scaffolding each other's reading. Heads together, fingers pressed to the page, readers process text in tandem, each supplying a word or phrase as they are able, constructing text together word by word, phrase by phrase, hinting, assisting, encouraging, talking, playing with language, discussing stories, and making the kinds of personal connections that thoughtful mature readers do:

- "Try that again."

- "If we read it fast it might sound better."

- "What if we saw the monster, would he get us?"

- "It starts with the same sound as your name."

- "I'm the jet. Watch me fly!"

- "Just cover the last part and do this part first."

Young readers scaffold one another's learning in an infinite variety of ways, developing child-centered strategies that respond to their learning needs and preferences. Although we may not abdicate our role as teachers, it is also our job to listen and learn as child partners help each other. We then take this knowledge and use it to plan minilessons and whole- or small-group discussions highlighting children's scaffolding strategies.

In peer partnerships, readers assist each other by their presence and camaraderie. Although they most often "tell the word," partners also offer scaffolds to move the reader forward.

For example, Pete gives an orthographic hint as he and Bobby read *The Tiny Woman's Coat* (Cowley 1987) together. When Bobby pauses on the word *take*, Pete hints *t-t-t*. Bobby then reads the line successfully: "Take some of our seeds, said the wild, w-w-wet weeds." Pete's hint has provided a quick scaffold that allows Bobby to decode the word—and another later in the sentence—himself.

Peer partners also give semantic hints. As Sam struggles with the word *time*, Sarah gives both an orthographic and semantic cue when she says, *"T-t-t . . .* like a clock."

Children also help one another by suggesting reading strategies, discussing and recommending book choices, and celebrating literacy accomplishments. When Bobby struggles, continually losing his place in a difficult text, Pete suggests, "Why don't you use your finger?" Later, after Sarah has read a storybook successfully, Bobby tells her, "You should take that one home."

■ Student Modeling and Demonstration

Children are powerful models as they demonstrate responsible partner behavior for their peers. Children love to teach their classmates, and students often listen to these demonstrations with fresher ears than they would a teacher demonstration. Once partnerships are established and children have listened to one or two demonstrations, they often ask if they may teach the group.

Some of the most successful student demonstrations I've observed focus on how to take turns and how to help when a partner does not know a word, but, as with teacher demonstrations, the possibilities are infinite. The strategies we highlight and encourage should be ones that the group or individuals need at the time. A few ideas for student demonstrations or modeling are:

1. *Voice volume.* Partners demonstrate how to use quiet, "five-inch" voices.

2. *What to do when a partner loses her place.* Partners rehearse and then demonstrate supportive ways to refocus one's partner.

3. *Taking turns.* Partners model different ways of taking turns—reading alternate pages, for example, or reading chorally.

4. *Selecting and returning books.* Partners model how they select and return books to browsing boxes or the classroom library. They also discuss why they choose certain books.

5. *Writing about partner reading.* In writing we discover what we think, enabling us to return to tasks with new understanding and insight. Writing about partner collaborations could include one's thoughts, feelings, or opinions about partner reading or rules for partner reading to post on classroom walls. *Great Grouping Strategies* (Wrubel 2002) has several ideas for partner reading response sheets. Appendices E, F, and G contain reading response sheets especially designed for peer partners.

I consider my demonstrations and those of my students to have been successful when I observe partners and solo readers applying them independently or hear the strategies being discussed in whole-group discussions.

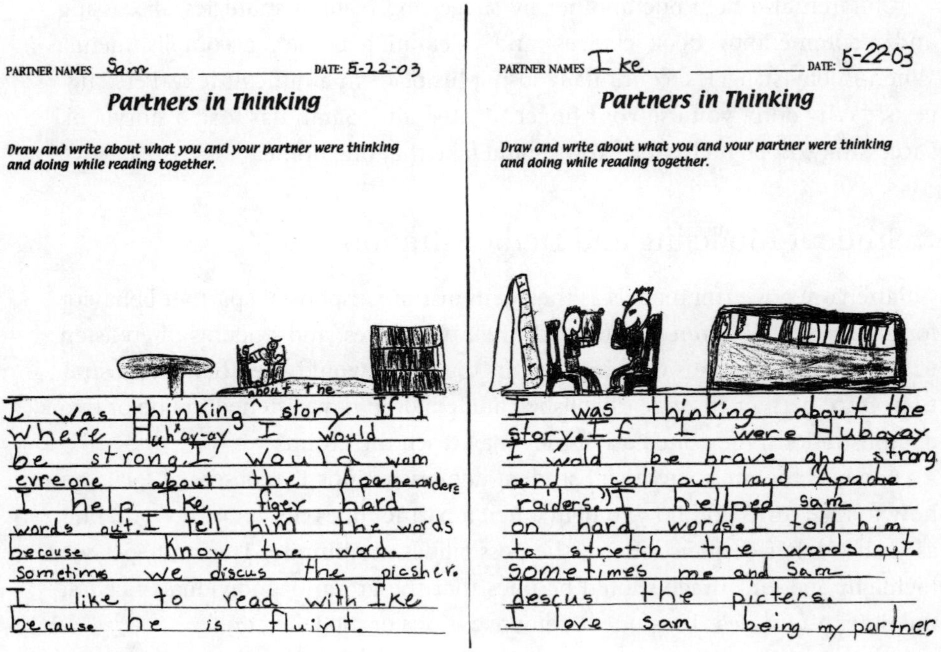

PARTNER NAMES **Sam** _____ DATE: **5-22-03**

Partners in Thinking

Draw and write about what you and your partner were thinking and doing while reading together.

I was thinking ^about the story. If I
Where Hub'ay-ay I would
be strong. I would warn
evreone about the Apache raiders
I help Ike tiger hard
words out. I tell him the words
because I Know the word.
Sometims we discus the picsher.
I like to read with Ike
because he is fluint.

PARTNER NAMES **Ike** _____ DATE: **5-22-03**

Partners in Thinking

Draw and write about what you and your partner were thinking and doing while reading together.

I was thinking about the
story. If I were Hubayay
I wold be brave and strong
and call out loud "Apache
raiders." I helped Sam
on hard words. I told him
to stretch the words out.
Sometimes me and Sam
descus the picters.
I love Sam being my partner.

FIG. 6–1 *Partners in thinking response*

■ Sharing Effective Strategies

When I make time for discussions in which students share their ideas about collaboration, I observe an immediate boost in reader confidence and independence. These discussions also give all students access to child-created strategies. Children's voices describing the kinds of things they do to support each other are the building blocks of my most effective, relevant teaching. The ways children tell me that they learn best, the ways they prefer to be helped, and the ways they have devised to help others are those things I most try to replicate in my teaching:

- "If I get stuck on a word, she gives me a clue, like look at the picture, or look for a little word in the big word. I would tell her to sound it out or look at the pictures to find a clue."

- "I skip, then he tells me the word sometimes, and I would start the sentence over and include that word. That's what my mom does."

- "He helps me track along and makes sure I don't make a mistake."

- "If she gets stuck on a word, I would tell her, 'You know this part of the word. I know you do!'"

- "I could just tell him there's a cluster in the beginning, if there was one."

- "My partner is my friend."

When I ask first graders how they help their partner or prefer to be helped, their responses often reflect their interest in reading words accurately. Of the hundreds of first graders I have interviewed over the past several years, over 50 percent mention "helping to sound out words" as an important partner strategy; almost as many mention "telling the word." Children also tell me that partners (themselves or others) should help or scaffold each other by using the following strategies.

- Point to the word.

- Tell their partner to "read fair" (take turns).

- Tell their partner to look for a cluster.

- Tell their partner to look for a chunk.

- Tell their partner to skip to see what makes sense, then take another look.

- Tell their partner to look for a vowel.

- Listen.

- Give the first letter/sound.

- Help spell the word.

- Tell their partner to look at the picture, then back at the word.

- Pronounce the unfamiliar word for their partner.

- Stretch the unfamiliar word out like a rubber band.

- Give a sound like *eh-eh-eh* for a word with a short *e*.

- Help their partner solve a word he doesn't know.

- Tell their partner to break the word apart, like *be–cause*.

- Take turns.

- Be quiet.

- Frame the word with their fingers.

- Track along with each letter.

- Hint.

- Say, "It starts with the first letter of my name."

- Help their partner recognize the silent *e*.

- Give a hint like *animal* if the word is *horse*.

- Tell their partner to look for a little word in the big word.

- Help their partner read with expression (notice punctuation).

- Help their partner read loud when the text is very black (boldface).

- Tell their partner to use the strategies she knows.

- Make sure their partner has a good time.

These responses reflect the teaching and modeling these young readers have experienced in literate classrooms. They demonstrate attention to all the cueing systems: semantic, syntactic, and orthographic. They also reflect paying sustained attention to the flow of the story and what it means.

When they put their heads together, beginning readers support and assist each other by:

- talking about text and illustrations

- offering verbal cues

- using nonverbal cues (gestures)

- suggesting ways to organize the task and the environment

- making decisions about books

Talking About Text and Illustrations

If expectations are clear, emergent reading partners are task-oriented, their talk focused on the text and illustrations. For example, Mark and Jerry are reading a page that says, "This is where OUR plants will grow." Jerry reads, "This is where our plants will grow." Mark points to the word *OUR*, written in capital letters:

"No, you have to say it BIGGER!" Jerry rereads, "This is where OUR plants will grow."

Observing countless peer partnerships over the years, I have rarely found that partners' talk pulls them off task. Rather than distracting readers, peer partners' talk more often helps them organize their reading while keeping both partners involved. My research also suggests that partner talk creates and supports the "shared situations" necessary for scaffolding and assistance, whether readers are discussing a word, suggesting a book, exploring illustrations, or sharing background knowledge with each other.

Partners also question and conjecture, bringing their personal stances to the text. As they discuss and explore pictures and print, partners imagine they are stepping into the story, as is illustrated in the following interaction between Bobby and Pete as they read *The Hogboggit* (Bowes 1985):

Bobby	**Pete**
The hogboggit roars at me. Can you imagine . . . if it roars at you?	
	I would hit him on the head with a hammer.
It's a shadow, you can't. *I roar louder! The hogboggit is running away. I . . .* [pauses] . . . *think it is scared.* [Turns the page] *It has gone!*	
	It was only a candle, right? [The picture shows a girl holding a candle]
No, it was only near a candle, so it would make a shadow.	

Bobby and Pete question, clarify, and confirm. Rather than detracting from the reading, this talk seems to involve each child more deeply in the process. The book is Bobby's selection, and while he reads most of this short predictable text, Pete is very focused and involved throughout. From the beginning of the story, illustrations clearly indicate that the hogboggit is nothing more than the girl's shadow, yet the boys make many conjectures about the nature of the mysterious "monster." Pete's intentional but imaginative talk—"I would hit him on the head with a hammer"—reflects his personal and emotional response to the story and its dramatic illustrations.

Partners' talk, particularly instances of word play, reveal their thinking as they create and maintain their collaborative relationships. Partner talk often centers on pictures as readers use their background knowledge to explain or elaborate on text. In the interaction below, Bobby and Pete read *Big Egg* (Coxe

FIG. 6–2

1997), the story of a very large egg that lands in a hen's nest (inspiring both story characters' and readers' speculation about the kind of creature that will hatch from it):

Bobby

The small eggs [pauses on *crack*]

[Shrugs] *The small eggs . . . crack.* [Turns the page] *P–p–peep! Peep!*

Peep! Peep! . . . say the small chicks. [Turns the page and pauses, studying the word *squawk*] *Squ–squ–SQUAWK!*

chick.

ch–ch–chicken. That's not a chicken or a goose or an ostrich.

Pete

[Leans forward, studying the picture] Think it's a monster?

[Laughs] Peep, peep, peep, peep!

SQUAWK! SQUAWK! [Adds] Squawk, squawk,squawk . . . *says the big duck* [for *chick*]

Bobby and Pete are constructing text and making meaning as they endeavor to maintain fluency. Their focus shifts repeatedly from print to pictures as they make predictions, conjectures, and comments concerning the narrative. They also read and play with the simple repetitive language of this beginning reader story.

Verbal Cueing

Verbal cueing is the scaffold most often modeled and encouraged by teachers and most often mentioned by students when creating charts of strategies about "how to help my partner." If a reader is stuck on a word, we ask children to hint, rather than tell the word, giving them many ideas for kinds of hints:

- Give the first sound.

- Tell them to read on to see what makes sense.

- Wait and give your partner time to think.

We also ask partners to notice textual road signs such as punctuation or sentence boundaries and to help each other use these signs to construct text and make meaning.

However, what partners do in the heat of the moment depends on *their needs* and may not necessarily reflect our modeling. For example, Aaron and Norman are reading *How to Ride a Giraffe* (Cary 1995). Norman pauses, unsure of the word *tickle*. Aaron reads, "T-t-t i-i-i tick tickle!"

Successful collaborators view reading together as a challenge to be approached together. As Joe says, "When you don't know the words and they do, they help you solve the problem." As children read in tandem, they call on all kinds of verbal strategies to support and scaffold each other:

- "She gives me a hint . . . like it begins like my name."

- "He tells me if I get mixed up."

- "There are lots of tricky words that partners can read together."

- "He tells me where to read."

- "She shows me a little word that I know."

Nonverbal Cueing (Gestures)

Peer reading partners use many kinds of nonverbal cueing to scaffold each other's learning, especially pointing and eye signals. Nonverbal cues often serve multiple functions for the emergent reader, functions that help broaden the definition of reading to encompass much more than simply "saying the words on the page."

Pointing

Pointing, in particular, is an important communication and collaboration tool for paired readers. Partners point to help each other keep their place or focus more closely on text. Readers usually point with their index finger, occasionally using an open hand with all fingers under a line of text. They also point with closed fist or sometimes an object such as a small pointer, pencil, or rolled-up paper tube. For example, Carol reads, "'Plants will not grow here," said Cat. "It's so dry. It's [for *This*] is not where plants grow.'" Vera points to *This*. Carol rereads correctly. "This is not where plants grow." Vera nods and smiles, her eyes focused on the text.

When readers struggle with unfamiliar words, pointing is sometimes introduced as a tool to scaffold decoding, either by providing extra focus on the word or as an aid in left–right processing. For example, in a paired reading, Emma pauses on the word *shivering*. Her partner Kitty leans closer and points. She continues to point as both readers study the word. Kitty reads, "Sh . . . sh. . . ." Emma reads, "Sh . . . shiv . . . shuh . . . shivering!" A reading partner might also run a finger slowly under the word or cover part of the word to focus reader's attention on one syllable at a time.

Another common function of pointing is to signal turn taking at the start of a new page of text. When used in this way, pointing is often accompanied by eye contact or a verbal cue—"your turn" or "you read." A few other nonverbal ways I have observed partners indicate a switch in whose turn it is are nudging, poking, tapping, flapping the book up and down, or waving the book in the partner's face.

Sometimes partners use pointing to control the reading. For example, after reading, one partner may continue to point even if it is no longer her turn, refusing to relinquish this role to the reader. Occasionally, the nonreading partner points alongside the reader's hand or on top of it. This more aggressive, controlling type of pointing is sometimes met with complacence by the partner, sometimes actively rebuffed, the reader either pushing the pointer's hand away or giving a verbal cue—"No"; "Take your hand away"; "Your hand's bothering me." Children often solve the problem of excessive or controlling pointing themselves, but I try to observe and listen, stepping in if they need help. At such times, I usually redirect the reader or gather the group together to lead a discussion about appropriate kinds of pointing.

Eye signals

Eye signals also serve many functions. Children make eye contact to seek help and to indicate taking turns, the latter usually but not always accompanied by a verbal cue or pointing. Children also use eye signals to resist or rebuff a partner's help and to give the partner a nonverbal cue that her or his behavior is unacceptable. Sometimes, readers use eye signals to indicate fatigue or exasperation with the reading, rolling their eyes or opening them wide. This type of eye signal often begins as an individual gesture, but it becomes public when the partner notices.

Do teachers need to talk about pointing and eye signaling? Perhaps not, since both kinds of behavior are modeled continuously during instruction. Being aware of their function as learner scaffolds, however, helps me highlight supportive uses of nonverbal cues and gestures when I observe them, as well as discourage nonverbal gestures that detract or infringe on peer partner collaboration. Also, I am always working to educate myself about the meaning different cultures place on nonverbal behavior. I want to be aware of the "silent language" (Hall 1981) I use when I teach, model, and interact with children.

Helping Organize Task and Environment

Most adults have difficulty functioning or completing tasks if they feel scattered or disorganized. Therefore, organizational strategies are important components of learner-to-learner scaffolding. Partners help each other stay organized in many ways:

- suggesting ways to take turns

- locating one's place on the page

- keeping materials sorted and ready to use

Readers also assume roles within the partnership that allow reading to proceed smoothly and fairly:

- "Hey, you skipped a page. Here's where to start."

- "We take a book, each read a page, then switch."

- "Take books out of bags and put 'em like this. Pick one and read. Put book back in bag and pick another."

- "Elizabeth's the leader today, and she goes first. Tomorrow, it's my turn."

When I ask Sharon Roberts about her students' organizational behavior in peer partnerships, she says, "They would say 'I'm on this page' or 'You're on that page.' Or they would do some kind of tapping and pointing when it was their partner's turn and the partner was not aware, subtle things like that. Very seldom did I see a child get so upset with her partner that they had to call for my intervention. They seem to have a way of communicating with each other that I don't need to know." We cannot and perhaps should not know everything readers are doing in partnership. We do, however, need to respect their communications about structure and organization as valuable insights into beginning readers' definitions of collaboration.

Making Decisions About Books

Even with lots of modeling, book selection can be a daunting task for young readers. Through whole-class discussions and guided reading, we continually model for children how to introduce themselves to books and how to choose books that match their interests as well as their reading level. Peer partners who know each other's interests and capabilities can help each other find a just-right book on a given day. Partners also work together to select books that are just right for the partnership:

- "If you're not sure what to read, the person next to you knows. They can say 'That's a just-right book,' and you can read it."

- "You should take that book home. You read it really good."

- "Me and Freddie like *Down by the Bay* (Westcott 1988). We can sing it like Raffi and it's fun."

■ Summing Up

As Tyler and I sit down for his interview, I notice that his arm is in a cast. "I fractioned it," he explains, going on to relate the story of how he fractured his wrist the day before and had to miss school. When we return to the subject of partner reading, he says, "It's like we're brothers reading together, because we're reading each other stuff, and I don't like reading alone. You have their company." Tyler mentions over and over how partners are like brothers and tells me at one point, "I help him, that's what brothers do." He goes on to say that he had a brother once, but he died. I later learn from his teachers that he indeed had a twin brother, who died when Tyler was two.

No matter how many "programs" we throw at children, reading remains a deeply personal act. Tyler's thoughts, echoed by many first graders, attest to the significance young children place on these social relationships. Listening to Tyler, it is difficult to regard partner reading as simply "filler" between the activities that comprise the "real work of the classroom." Not only does Tyler appreciate his partner's reading help, he also sees him as a brother in a relationship characterized by support and trust.

Kristen Vito says, "Giving kids control will only further your work and your program." When children are given many models of effective literacy strategies and then trusted to choose the structures and strategies that work best for them, they are quite capable of having meaningful, rich interactions over text. These interactions, seen as part of a larger whole, contribute to building a trusting, supportive classroom community. Children's responsiveness to one another is revealed not only in their language play and organizational talk but also in their willingness to step aside and make a place for partners to act, learn, and grow. Students' talk continually contributes to the intersubjective whole created within social relationships focused on reading.

When young readers work together, they pool cognitive resources, each contributing to the task as they are able. Not all interactions are positive. Certain children have great difficulty sharing and collaborating, particularly at the start of the school year. Helping partners develop collaborative skills ensures that all readers will have access to these supportive contexts.

Children assist and scaffold one another's learning through verbal and non-verbal behavior learned and developed within the context of comprehensive literacy programs. Although they appropriate many strategies and skills emphasized in their classroom reading programs, peer partners take particular pride in the original strategies they develop together, generously sharing these strategies with classmates through discussion and modeling. Teachers must also suggest and model forms of assistance readers might try, soliciting children's ideas about tools and strategies they use to support one another. Making time for readers to construct or develop tools together, planning and structuring contexts that nurture young readers, then stepping back to allow readers to construct text on their own terms, are key teaching elements that support effective *independent* partnerships.

7 | Building Skills and Strategies

Each year, teachers plan and implement peer partnerships according to the needs and interests of their students and literacy programs. Many teachers, I among them, use partnerships to support and encourage "almost independent" reading. Others use them for practice, asking children to reread familiar text. Buddy reading is often a center activity. Peer partnerships can also be ideal contexts for strengthening and deepening children's comprehension and fluency skills as partners discuss and question the message conveyed by both print and illustrations, arriving at shared meaning through their collaborative talk.

Children express an overwhelming preference for buddy reading over reading alone. As David, a first grader, says, "Buddies are friendly and they help if I get stuck. If they get stuck, I help them, too, 'cause I know a lot of words." Teachers, taking valuable cues from children's love of partner reading, seek ways to incorporate this model into all kinds of literacy programs.

■ Using Peer Partnerships to Build Fluency

Many teachers use peer partnerships as a way for young readers to practice and strengthen their fluency skills and strategies. In the company of supportive "buddies," students read longer and more expressively, sustaining their involvement in texts as they work with concepts or ideas that might prove too challenging or defeating to tackle alone. In thinking about how to strengthen readers' fluency in partnerships, I ask the following questions.

PARTNER NAMES Rosie _____ DATE: 5-22-03

Partners in Thinking

Draw and write about what you and your partner were thinking and doing while reading together.

I like Budy redding because we can read to gether. We can get flooint in reading. If we Budy read we can all lem more and more beter werd choice. We lem more werds to write on popper. When I read with my friends I becum a beter reader!

FIG. 7–1 *Rosie's thinking*

Building Skills and Strategies ■ ■ ■ **77**

- What minilessons can I provide that will encourage children to read more fluently?

- Is fluency more than simply reading the words accurately and quickly? What about punctuation? How is meaning conveyed by the way I read and how can I help children see this?

- If fluency is the primary goal, is hinting better than quickly helping one's partner over a rough spot?

- Is choral reading better than alternating pages if the goal is to encourage and support fluent reading?

- What kinds of books encourage partners' fluency? patterned? repetitive? song lyrics? poems?

I model fluent reading during read-alouds and shared reading. I also reread small snippets of text in different ways, asking children to tell me which sounds best or which makes the most sense.

Although simply reading with a partner encourages fluency, some specific ideas for peer reading partnerships follow:

1. *Rereading favorite texts.* Partners reread stories and other texts previously heard or read during read-alouds, shared reading, or guided reading. Big books are often favorite texts for partners to read together.

2. *Rereading as the character.* If a story has clearly defined characters with lots of dialogue, ask children to reread a familiar story, each taking a character's part throughout. For reading like this, children can also create simple props, such as puppets or masks. (Jan Brett's website, *www.janbrett.com,* has wonderful puppets and masks to use with her stories.)

3. *Singing stories.* Gather storybooks based on favorite children's songs, and encourage children to sing stories.

4. *Reading interpretatively.* Ask partners to select small segments of "meaningful text" and read, reread, and practice "in the way the author intended." Later, when the class meets as a whole, partners can share or perform these expressive, interpretative readings.

Peer partnerships clearly support readers' fluent, sustained, and meaningful enjoyment of text. If fluency is my goal for students, I try to tread lightly when I intervene in peer reading interactions. I also consider carefully how strict I want to be in insisting that peer partners use my rules about hinting and holding back instead of rules they devise together. Finally, many of the activities in *Fluency in Focus: Comprehension Strategies for All Young Readers* (Prescott-Griffin & Witherell 2004) can be adapted and used to build readers' fluency in peer partnerships.

■ Using Peer Partnerships to Build Comprehension

Many teachers use partner reading to build comprehension skills and strategies, believing that once readers learn and practice skills and strategies in collaboration, they will use them more effectively when reading alone, whether that be stories, nonfiction, or items on a state or district reading assessment.

We live in a test-crazy, high-stakes world in which schools' and teachers' effectiveness and competence are judged by student outcomes on standardized state and district assessments. First-grade teachers like Sharon Roberts use peer partnerships as important vehicles for strengthening students' comprehension, "building their criteria for success" in predicting what's coming next, drawing conclusions and inferences, retelling stories, and discussing characters' motivations. She sees a direct relationship between this collaborative work, her students' understanding of stories, and their performance on district reading assessments. "Without the time to practice with partners, they'd never be prepared. They need the time together. You can't get this as effectively in small or whole groups. Kids need to be in the thick of it."

Standardized assessments aside, comprehension lies at the heart of reading and is its primary purpose and ultimate goal. For a variety of reasons, understanding is difficult for readers of all ages, and teachers must continually find ways to engage students' active thinking about text. Peer partnerships are ideal contexts for reading, sharing, and discussing text.

When collaborating, peer partners often make personal connections to the stories they read together. They notice features of text and discuss them, which helps group members read with expression: "They put black, black words—dark words—big words—so you can say them real loud." Readers step into books, imagining that they are the characters, living the experiences: "If I read about a carnival, I think I'm in the carnival, you know, like in the book." Partners also question and examine text with buddies, using their own knowledge to analyze the message.

The following activities and strategies encourage active reader engagement and strengthen comprehension skills as children step into text, examine and retell stories, discuss literary elements of stories, and explore text structures.

1. *Retell a story.* Partners read or reread a story, then retell it.

2. *Be the character.* Partners read or reread a story, then take parts and retell or act out the story. These performances can be shared with the whole group, or one partnership can perform for another.

3. *Create a story map.* After reading or rereading a story, partners create or fill in a "story map" outlining facets of story. The appendices include several examples. Karen D'Angelo Bromley's book *Webbing with Literature* (1991) has many more! Appendices H, I, J, and K present story map ideas that focus on character traits and motivations and plot elements. These maps can be a joint writing project or partners can complete individual maps, conferring with each other throughout the process.

4. *Use graphic organizers.* After reading a nonfiction text, partners collaborate, organizing and sorting relevant information on a graphic organizer or chart. See Appendices L and M for examples.

5. *Compare and contrast.* After or during reading, peer partners compare and contrast elements of text, creating written lists, Venn diagrams, or other charts that organize traits and sort characteristics. Possibilities are endless and include:

   - listing likes and dislikes (words, characters, situations)
   - categorizing and comparing kinds of species in a nonfiction text such as *Great Snakes!* (Robinson 1996) or *Amazing Lizards!* (Robinson 1999)
   - comparing and contrasting characters in a story—for example, using the picture book *Miss Nelson Is Missing* (Allard and Marshall 1977) to compare and contrast the sweet, patient Miss Nelson and the wicked, short-tempered, Miss Viola Swamp

6. *Extend the story.* After reading or rereading, partners discuss what they know about characters, plot, and situations and ask themselves, "If you were the author and wanted to write one more page or chapter, what would you write?"

7. *Investigate cause and effect.* Ask partners to read or reread a book such as *If You Give a Mouse a Cookie* (Numeroff 1985) or others in this delightful series and discuss cause and effect.

   - What happens when you give a mouse a cookie?
   - What caused the meatball to roll away? What caused it to turn into a tree?

8. *Identify the main idea and supporting details.* Ask partners to read and reread a story then discuss what it was "mainly about."

- How do you know this?
- What details can you find and list to support your conclusions about the main idea?

▪ Using Peer Partnerships to Build Community

It is early morning and Anne Santoro's students retrieve book bags, find a reading partner, and begin reading. Anne does not assign "buddies" but specifies that children must read with a member of their guided reading group. David and Thomas sit on the "math rug" under the windows. Each holds a copy of *Rosie's Pool* (Riley 1995). Thomas is reading, while David looks over his shoulder, reading along silently.

Thomas	David
She looked up and . . . s . . . [pauses on *saw*]	
	saw
saw three giants. They had come to visit her.	
[On page 6, the text reads, *Rosie asked the first giant, "Would you like to sit down?"*]	
	[Laughs, pointing to the picture of the giant] Look, that guy has a stringy mustache!
[Laughs] *"Why don't you sit down?"*	
	[Laughs and points to the illustration] He's already sitting on the chair!
[On page 7, the text reads: *"How nice," he said. "Thank you." "You're welcome," said Rosie.*]	
"How nice," he said. "Thank you." "You're . . ." [Pauses on *welcome*]	
	welcome!
[Nods] *"You're welcome," said Rosie.*	

Thomas continues to read through *Rosie's Pool,* while David listens, offering assistance, usually by telling a word when Thomas is unsure. These partners chuckle, point to the illustrations, and talk about various aspects of the story, most often the silly things the giants are doing. After the book is finished, it is David's turn. He selects a book from his book bag and Thomas assumes the role of listener.

David and Thomas are deeply immersed in jointly reading text. Whether in the role of reader or listener, both view this time as a collaboration, as they enjoy and construct text in tandem. No matter who is reading, the listener is attentive and supportive, never usurping the task but lending assistance as needed.

Anne sees the purpose of partner reading as "twofold, as a peer tutorial and as a way for students to cue into each other, really listen to each other." She also values these collaborations because the skills and strategies children develop "really help them work together at other times." Anne's students have many things to say about why they like buddy reading. A number, like Betsy, talk about the social aspects of partner reading: "Because if I were to be alone, I'd be by myself, and I don't like to be by myself, because when I was by myself and I didn't know a word, there was no one to help. My friend helps me."

Children often mention friendship when they talk about reading with a buddy, a friendship that has originated from the reading partnership, a friendship that supports their literate understanding, a friendship that means they are not alone. When asked why she likes reading with a partner, Sally says, "'Cause it's comfortable and fun. 'Cause you sit in a chair and read to a friend."

■ Using Peer Partnerships in Literacy Centers

In some classrooms, pairing readers of approximately equal expertise is challenging, as center work is often undertaken by heterogeneous groups. Anne Santoro resolves this dilemma by using several types of buddy reading throughout the school day. In the early morning, children pair with a member of their guided reading group; later, when working in centers, they partner with a reader who is often at a very different level of literacy development. To accommodate these differences, Anne and her students are more flexible about choosing center reading material. Often center buddies choose to "read the room," revisiting familiar poems, chart stories, and other shared print. Center buddies also take turns reading whole texts from their book bags, so each has the opportunity to read books at his or her level.

Jenny Baumeister and her colleagues plan heterogeneous reading partnerships as a regular classroom center. Like Anne, Jenny finds other times during the day for peer partner reading to "get them reading at similar independent levels and build fluency."

When she first introduces buddy reading as a center activity, Jenny models the behavior she expects from partners. Jenny and a student sit side by side, and the group discusses why this is important when reading in partnership. The teacher–student team then demonstrates reading alternate pages and reading chorally, using quiet voices. Later, Jenny asks partnerships to try both ways of taking turns, but they are free to choose the method that works best for them.

Jenny tells students that she expects listening partners to "be good listeners and to look at the person reading." She stresses the importance of paying attention and "not moving around while your partner is reading." These expectations, appropriate for this group of children, might look somewhat different with another group. Christi Walsh, one of Jenny's fellow first-grade teachers, models questions partners can ask each other during and after reading in the buddy reading center. Both teachers expect children to "use their strategies":

- Look at pictures.

- Really think about meaning.

- Look closely at letter patterns.

■ Using Peer Partnerships in Buddy Circles

Joy Richardson uses three types of peer partnerships in her classroom. Her goals for all three structures center around building her students' reading fluency, confidence, and enjoyment. At the beginning of the year, students sometimes pair up to reread stories in the reading series the district has adopted. They also read with buddies at the buddy reading center. After students have practiced buddy reading during these activities, Joy begins buddy circles midyear. Originally, she began buddy circles to support a child who was very undisciplined when reading independently. Joy says, "When he reads with buddies, he feels more comfortable. Before, he'd pick a book off the shelf, look at the first page, and if he couldn't read the first word, that was it. He gave up for the entire reading workshop. With buddies, he sticks with it. He likes reading to friends."

Joy also sees value in children rereading books a number of times. "They notice things. They make connections with the characters. They make connections between stories, themes, ideas, and characters." She also finds that rereading helps students ask better questions about the books because "they really know them." Finally, Joy says that buddies "stay on each other and keep each other on track and on task."

Joy's class begins the day with journal writing and sharing. Joy then meets with guided reading groups. While Joy works with a guided reading group, the remainder of the students work in buddy circles made up of members of their guided reading group. Buddy circle routines are clear and well established. Following snack, children retrieve their book bags and bring them to their circle. The plastic self-sealing bags contain five to eight books that children have read previously during guided reading. Group members select which book to read

FIG. 7–2

and begin. Some groups read by alternating pages, while other groups read chorally. Still others alternate between these turn-taking options throughout the session.

One buddy circle of five children gathers on a small carpeted area near Joy's guided reading table. They decide to read *The Secret Room* (Hunt & Brychta 1992), and everyone pulls a copy of the book from her or his book bag. As Terry opens her book and begins reading, Kate says, "No! This page," and points to the opposite page. Kate then proceeds to read that page; Terry reads the next one. The others follow, each reading one page, moving clockwise around the circle. This is a familiar book and children read easily without miscue.

Terry reads, "Mom and Dad put [for *pulled*] the wallpaper off." Kate reaches over and points to *pulled* in Terry's book. Terry rereads correctly, "Mom and Dad pulled the wallpaper off" and the children continue reading smoothly through page 15, when Sam reads, "It looks like. . . ." Dennis interrupts, saying "It LOOKS!" indicating that Sam should read with expression. Sam rereads, "'It LOOKS like our house,'" said Mom.

At this point, the group takes a few minutes to discuss the pictures and point to and identify characters (Mom, Dad, Chip, and Bobbie, the sister) before continuing. Dennis reads expressively, followed by Sam who reads softly, but without miscue. As Sam finishes, Kate says, "Louder!" Sam rereads a little louder. The group continues taking turns until the end. As they choose a new book,

Kate says, "How 'bout we go around the circle [each taking a turn] till the last page?" Her buddies nod and they begin the new story.

Kate acts as this group's director, keeping them on task and moving forward. She structures how they will read and corrects and monitors her buddies' reading. For the most part, the group cedes control to Kate, and they remain productively engaged throughout the forty-five-minute period. Around the room, other groups organize somewhat differently. Some read chorally, others take turns as Kate's group has done. No matter how they organize and structure their time, however, all groups have a director or leader. This is not something Joy has required or suggested, but something that has evolved based on group needs.

Organizing Buddy Circles

Buddy circle members negotiate structures that allow them to work cooperatively, giving everyone a chance to read and direct. All buddy circle members take turns selecting the book. Frequently, the person who selects the book begins the reading, either by initiating a group choral reading or reading the first page, then ceding the task to the reader beside her, and so on around the circle. Some groups change leaders with each new book. Other groups retain the same leader for days or weeks. Either way, each child eventually has the opportunity to lead the reading.

Members of buddy circles usually begin reading with little fanfare, so that most of the time is spent reading: "Put your books like this [fanning them out, flat on the table], then pick." They help each other by keeping track of whose turn it is, so that reading encounters are fair and equitable: "I went last to pick the book today, so I go first tomorrow." As with other classroom routines, children have a clear understanding of their task and responsibility: "We get books out. We all choose the same book, then we start reading. We go around in a circle."

Supporting Buddy Circles

Joy supports peer partnerships and buddy circles by "lots of modeling and discussion about responsible group behavior." When she first opens the buddy reading center she models and discusses appropriate buddy behavior, then frequently reminds children about how they are to behave. She also encourages children to give hints rather than telling the word when a reader struggles. To support and promote positive group strategies, Joy tries to "debrief" after buddy circles, asking children what went well and what they might like to try differently next time. During these debriefing sessions, Joy might also highlight positive behavior or suggest peer reading strategies to children.

Although Joy's first graders mostly help one another with word solving, they have also developed creative, meaningful ways to spark one another's thinking: "I help 'em sound it out. Then if they still don't get it, I ask, 'Do we sing a song with that word in it?'" They also echo Joy's recommendations on how to best help a reader with an unfamiliar word: "I say the first sound—the beginning one—or if there's a chunk in the middle." Supporting young readers' word-solving strategies during group minilessons and strategy discussions contributes to the success of these small-group interactions.

Joy has high expectations for her students' behavior and academic engagement. Her voice and manner are calm, quiet, reassuring, and respectful, and the children's behavior reflects her example. Students are self-motivated and view themselves as readers and writers. They make a smooth transition from home to school through journal writing and extend their literate pursuits responsibly and independently into buddy circles.

Although each teacher should plan and implement buddy circles according to the social, emotional, and cognitive needs of the students, here are some suggestions.

- Develop students' collaborative skills in pairs before moving to the small-group model.

- Plan to spend at least part of the first few days or weeks of buddy circles checking in with each group before using that time to work with guided reading groups.

- Introduce group discussions in which you can articulate your expectations and students can share and suggest effective buddy circle strategies.

Appreciating Buddy Circles

When asked how they feel about reading in buddy circles, Joy's students' responses reflect their appreciation for the support and benefits of reading with peers. Robbie says, "If you make a mistake, there's someone there to help you." Reading with buddies enhances their enjoyment and increases their motivation. As Rosie says, "When you're with buddies, you're together. It's more fun to read and be together." The children clearly see buddies as helping them improve their reading. Cathy says, "It helps you be a better reader; if you keep reading, it will make reading a lot softer." They also see buddy reading as a way to process text more effectively: "When we read together, we get most of the words." Finally, these readers view buddy reading as supportive of their own individual development. Molly says, "It's fun when you read the same books over again. It helps you have fluency. You know, it's like when you're reading, like a talking mark or an exclamation point, you can read it with excitement. If there's shouting in the book, you can pretend you're that person and shout it out. Your partner helps you remember."

Joy's buddy circles help all her students develop fluency, confidence, and reading strategies. In describing this phenomenon, Joy mentions a shy, quiet girl who has blossomed as a reader in her buddy circle. "During guided reading, she's very shy and speaks very softly: you can't hear her. But I think with buddy reading, she's reading more and not feeling so insecure, because she's not in the spotlight."

■ Summing Up

Peer partnerships are very flexible. Partnerships are often "filler" between activities: teachers ask children to read with buddies when they have a few free minutes after completing reading and writing assignments, centers, or other classroom activities. Buddy reading can also be a calming transition from active parts of the school day such as recess or physical education, helping children refocus and ready themselves for the next academic activity.

If you are already using peer partnerships casually like this, I urge you to observe them closely and find ways to strengthen and enhance these literate interactions. Peer partnerships provide strong, collaborative contexts for talk and activities that build all young children's reading skills and strategies.

Working with a buddy also allows readers to share the sometimes daunting tasks we set before them. As Sharon Roberts says, "They like being with a buddy, because it takes the pressure off them personally, individually. With a buddy, they can be freer to enjoy the story, to have fun with it, to read smoothly and deepen their understanding while sharing the sometimes tricky task or assignment I have given them."

With a collaborator at their side, even very young children set to work reading text interpretively and exploring challenging concepts like main idea, cause and effect, and drawing inferences. Kristen Vito says, "I am always surprised by how much they get out of it—how they rise to the occasion and work to higher levels with their partners."

Through the strategies and structures children create, their behavior and language play, they reveal their imaginative approach to text and their interactive involvement with reading. In their very personal stances toward books, young readers bring teachers their perspectives on what it means to be truly literate (Griffin 2002). I urge you to pay attention to these perspectives and think about peer partnerships' role in young readers' literacy development. Planning ways that partnerships can strengthen fluency and comprehension, promote a lifelong love of reading, and enable children to practice and refine all reading skills allows these social interactions to be so much more than filler!

Providing Literature That Supports Collaboration

8

My favorite book to read with my partner is Chrysanthemum *[Henkes 1991] because you see the feeling that is happening when you read it together.*

When I'm with my partner, any book's a good book.

My partner knows the books I like, you know, the just-right ones that I can read. We pick 'em together, then we read, read, read.

Certain texts are particularly suited to reader collaboration. Finding the right book for the right child at the right moment is one of the real joys of teaching. Reading choices reflect personal interests, reader confidence, current passions. When children choose books to read together, they may pick the same kinds of books they read by themselves or they may use very different criteria. When I ask students what kind of books they read with their partners, most often they mention humor—funny situations, silly characters, rhyming words, engaging refrains. They also talk about plot, structure, personal connections and feelings, and the pleasure of reading about things they know: "I like to read about dads, 'cause my dad's always diggin', runnin', readin', swingin', swimmin', colorin', and sleepin'. Yup, he's busy."

In some classrooms, peer partners do not choose books, instead sharing familiar stories they have read previously during guided reading. In other classrooms, partners select books from browsing boxes, books that may or may not be familiar to them. There are also classrooms in which partners select from a wide range of choices, sometimes choosing text with many challenges, texts that

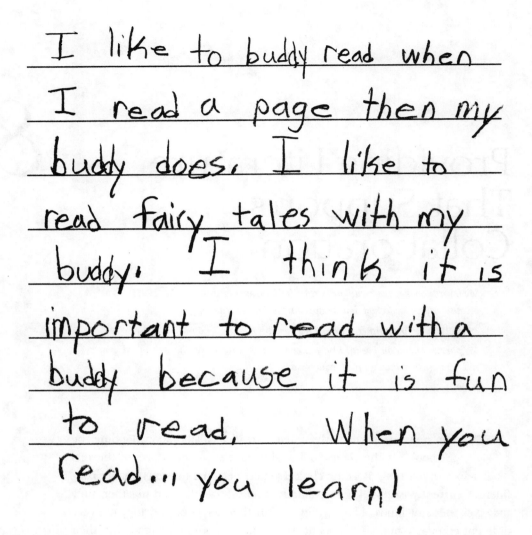

FIG. 8–1 *"I like to read with a buddy"*

they may be able to read only partially, even with the help of a strategizing partner.

When left to their own devices, peer partners' text choices range from easy to difficult, each chosen for different and distinct purposes. Often children initially select very easy books, singing or chanting their way through these selections as they warm up for more challenging books later in the session. They often read these warm-up books chorally, then read more challenging texts by alternating pages. In very challenging books, readers sometimes return to choral reading as they problem-solve their way through text line by line, their fingers tracking their progress. What partners do with text depends not only on the personalities involved, but also on the structure and qualities of the text.

We live in an amazing era of children's book publishing: there are thousands of supportive, engaging, beautiful books available for beginning readers. Young readers can find books on almost any subject—stories about all kinds of people, stories with imaginative, lively language and colorful illustrations. Even beginning chapter books, those most revered of texts, are available and accessible to primary-grade readers as they begin to get the hang of reading.

The literature categories I outline here are by no means inclusive, and you will no doubt think of many more categories of books to use with your students. One thing I know: For every book or series of books of which I am aware, there are hundreds, maybe thousands, of which I am not. The important thing is to keep searching and reading—at conferences, in libraries and bookstores—to find just-right books to put into children's hands at just-right moments. Some categories of books partners enjoy together are discussed in detail below.

■ Books Featuring Playful Language

"Spoooooky house. SQUAWK, SQUAWK, SQUAWK!" Children love to play with language, the magical rhythms and rhymes that roll off the tongue, in joyous, rollicking repetition—"Mr. Grump, Mr. Grump, Mr. Grump–grump–grump!" (Cowley 1987). They anticipate phrases and resolutions, and they delight in characters' words and actions: *The Little Red Hen (Makes a Pizza)* [Sturges 1999] is really good at the end, you know, when the animals all say, 'I have to eat the bread!' Now, that's funny."

Partners play with language by using funny voices (high, low, screechy), singing, drawling, and chanting, as well as by engaging in a great deal of playful talk related to pictures. Readers also engage in text-related play as they repeat choral patterns—"peep, peep, peep"—reinvent text, or elaborate on what is written or displayed in text illustrations. Language play evokes a number of partner responses, ranging from laughter and dancing to singing and shouting.

Books with repetitive choruses capture children's delight; they return to these texts again and again. Two examples are *Mr. Grump* (Cowley 1987) and *Noise* (Cowley 1987). In *Noise,* various objects—a radio, a television, a stereo—assail the characters with a cacophonic chorus ("yukka-dukka, yukka-dukka, yah, yah, yah") that many readers chant whenever there is a pause or break in text.

In addition to creating shared enjoyment, language play often refocuses or redirects a partner's wandering attention. Playfulness like this rarely diverts partners from the text for more than a minute, usually for no more than a few seconds, and it heightens interpersonal relationships and increases readers' interest in and enjoyment of stories. My research suggests that the interpersonal connections formed when playing with the language in such books as *Mr. Grump* enhance readers' success in processing or constructing more difficult text on which they *must* collaborate in order to be successful.

Book Suggestions

Big Egg (Coxe 1997)

Chicka Chicka Boom Boom (Martin & Archambault 1989)

The Little Red Hen (Makes a Pizza) (Sturges 1999)

Miss Mary Mac All Dressed in Black (Hastings 1990)

Mr. Grump (Cowley 1987)

Noise (Cowley 1987)

The Secret of Spooky House (Cowley 1987)

The Teeny Tiny Woman (O'Connor 1986)

■ Predictable and Patterned Books

The best patterned or predictable texts allow children to anticipate and "predict" what will happen on the next page and as the story comes to an end. Once readers become aware of the patterns, these texts support their independent reading. Young readers want their books to have patterns and designs they can follow. This is especially important when you read aloud for an audience, even an audience of one.

Book Suggestions

There are thousands and thousands of excellent predictable and patterned texts available from a wide variety of publishers. Here are just a few:

Berenstain Bears and the Spooky Old Tree (Berenstain & Berenstain 1978)

County Fair (Mayer 2002)

Five Little Monkeys Jumping on the Bed (Christelow 1989)

Good Night, Good Knight (Moore Thomas 2000)

I Can Draw (Medina 2000)

I Can Jump (Cowley 1986)

I Can Read (Williams 1994)

I Can Write (Williams 1994)

Mrs. Wishy-Washy (Cowley 1989)

My School (Peters 1995)

Oh, Cats! (Buck 1997)

Paul (Laurence 1992)

Ratty Tatty (Cowley 1987)

Billy Goats Gruff (Read It Yourself) (Hunia 1977)

The Sly Fox and The Red Hen (Read It Yourself) (Hunia 1977)

Goldilocks and the Three Bears (Read It Yourself) (Hunia 1977)

Snow Day (Mayer 2002)

The Stubborn Pumpkin (Geringer 1999)

Uncle Buncle's House (Cowley 1986)

Up in a Tree (Cowley 1986)

Will You Play with Me? (Phinney 1995)

Publishers of predictable and patterned series include:

Benchmark Education Company

Mondo Publishing

National Geographic

Newbridge Publishing

Oxford Blue and Red Readers

Pacific Learning

Pioneer Valley Educational Press

Rigby Publishing

Scholastic Publishing

Sundance Publishing

The Wright Group

■ Humorous Texts

Young readers seek humor everywhere. They choose books because they are funny, they write stories they hope will amuse, and they laugh together when plot twists take them by surprise. Amusing characters capture their attention, characters like Marc Brown's Arthur the Aardvark, whose human foibles and mishaps so closely resemble their own.

Most children's authors understand this about their readers and create wonderful stories laced with humor. Readers of all ages love to laugh, and they find all kinds of things to laugh about, from the absurd to the mundane, especially when they read side by side with a friend.

Book Suggestions

Arthur series (Marc Brown, various titles and dates)

Cinderella Dressed in Yellow (Williams 1994)

Clifford the Big Red Dog series (Bridwell)

I Spy Funny Teeth (Marzollo 2003)

Marvin One Too Many (Paterson 2001)

Mr. Grump (Cowley 1987)

Mrs. Brice's Mice (Hoff 1988)

Mrs. Wishy-Washy series (Cowley)

■ Song-Based Stories

Some peer partners love to sing and their singing supports and encourages their fluent reading of text. Pillows piled up beneath them, Pete and Freddie sit reading side by side in the class library nook. Freddie chooses the book *Down by the Bay* (Westcott 1988) and begins singing the text, Pete joining him in a joyful chorus that continues until the book's conclusion. Laughter punctuates their reading from time to time, but generally they remain focused and attentive to the text. Freddie then selects the book *Monkey Bridge* (Cowley 1987) and begins singing this text to the tune of *Down by the Bay.* His singing evolves into a kind of southern drawl as he reads on. Pete joins in on page 4.

A number of years ago, as I was preparing for my new class of first graders, I had a conversation with a kindergarten colleague about Pete, the child in the scenario above. Throughout kindergarten, Pete had struggled with reading readiness tasks and had already undergone extensive educational testing that labeled him "at risk" as an entering first grader. However, although he struggled with letters and sounds and small motor tasks, he knew the lyrics and tunes to hundreds of songs, from opera and show tunes to popular children's ditties.

Armed with this knowledge, I scoured bookstores, the Internet, and my local library searching for picture books based on children's songs. Using some of my yearly book money, my own funds, and my library card, I managed to collect over thirty "song books" suitable for beginning readers, with large print and lots of white space. Pete literally sang his way into reading using these song-based picture books and other patterned and predictable texts. He also wrote books of songs and performed them with his peers. His musical ear helped him develop reading and writing fluency.

Book Suggestions

Down by the Bay (Westcott 1998)

Five Little Ducks (Aruego & Dewey 1986)

Here We Go Round the Mulberry Bush (Hillenbrand 2003)

I Know an Old Lady Who Swallowed a Fly (Westcott 2003)

The Lady with the Alligator Purse (Westcott 1988)

Little Rabbit Foo Foo (Rosin & Robins 1990)

Miss Mary Mac All Dressed in Black: Tongue Twisters, Jump-Rope Rhymes, and Other Children's Lore from New England (Hastings 1990).

Old MacDonald Had a Farm (Alley 1991)

Seals on the Bus (Hart 2000)

Sitting Down to Eat (Harley 1996)

Skip to My Lou (Westcott 1988)

Wheels on the Bus (Wickstrom 1988)

Take Me Out of the Bathtub and Other Silly Dilly Songs (Katz 2001)

This Little Light of Mine (Lisberg 2003)

■ Poetry

Like other rhythmic, rhyming text, the language and patterns of poems are very supportive of young readers who are still "putting it all together." Many teachers teach a new poem (or two or three) every week. The poems are written out on chart paper so that all can see and read them. Poetry work is often completed in a poetry center. In some classrooms, learning, practicing, and illustrating poems happen at a regular time each week.

Poetry is a very important part of my reading program. My students learn a new poem every Friday. They each receive a copy of this poem to illustrate and take home and read to their family. Family members are encouraged to bind these poems into a book, keeping them handy to read again and again for practice and fluency. Chart paper containing poems lines my classroom walls, and a copy of each poem is placed in a Poetry Please notebook, which children can select to read independently or with partners. I also appoint a classroom "poetry person," who chooses poems to share at morning circle. Finally, whenever school funding allows, we hire "poets in residence" who visit and share their own writing and process while helping students write their own poems.

Book Suggestions

All the Small Poems (Worth 1987)

A Bug in the Teacher's Coffee and Other School Poems (Dakos 1999)

Honey, I Love and Other Love Poems (Greenfield 1978)

More Surprises (Bennett Hopkins 1987)

Nathanial Talking (Greenfield 1988)

Questions: Poems of Wonder (Bennett Hopkins 1992)

Seasons: A Book of Poems (Zolotow 2002)

Surprises (Bennett Hopkins 1984)

Weather: Poems for All Seasons (Bennett Hopkins 1994)

You Read to Me, I'll Read to You (Hoberman 2001)

■ Decodable Texts

Many teachers, including me, have collections of "decodable texts" in their classroom libraries. Although I neither advocate nor denounce the use of decodable texts, these books provide children with opportunities to focus on print. As such, they are resources for building readers' understanding about the alphabetic nature of language. Context in most decodable texts is limited and thus unengaging for all but the most diligent readers. Although a variety of decodable texts are always available to first graders in my classroom, children use only a few with any regularity, usually those with more engaging titles or with interesting cover illustrations. The three favorites are *The Jet* (Makar 1980), *Meg* (Makar 1995), and *Cop Cat* (Makar 1980).

I am often surprised when I watch children read decodable texts. Although certain books seem tedious, others provoke active, thoughtful joint construction. Children generally take turns in these texts, or sometimes read chorally. At no time have I ever observed a partner so carried away by the story that he read on, forgetting to give his partner a turn, a common occurrence when reading predictable, repetitive text.

Children's reading of decodable texts tends to be slow and plodding, and they often use a finger to keep their place or focus their partner's attention. Illustrations are limited, and the simple line drawings often fail to engage children's attention in the same way that the illustrations and photographs in most little books do. This sometimes leads to a breakdown in collaboration as listeners disengage or become just plain bored.

Each teacher must decide whether or not to make decodable texts available to readers. A few series of decodable texts suitable for beginning readers are listed below. These are given as resources but not recommended as a steady diet.

Book Suggestions

Phonetic Connections series (Benchmark Education)

Phonics for Reading series (Dominie Press)

Primary Phonics series (Educator's Publishing)

▪ Nonfiction

Many young readers prefer nonfiction. Fortunately, there has been an explosion in the publishing of excellent nonfiction for beginning readers. Using background knowledge and experience, partners explore nonfiction in different, often more critical ways than they do fiction.

"I like *How Long Do Animals Live?* [Braddock 2000] 'cause I can find out how long animals live. They made a mistake though. It says people live till seventy, but people live longer than seventy." What a heady sensation for readers of any age to discover that they know more than the printed text and how much more fun to make these discoveries with a partner, taking time to discuss and wonder about the author's "mistake."

The text structures of nonfiction present both challenge and support for readers of all levels. Once readers learn about structural conventions of nonfiction, they are able to use them to assist their exploration of text.

In selecting nonfiction for readers of any age, it is important to check for accuracy and clarity of writing. Although a few suggestions for nonfiction books and series are given below, you will want to search for those that best serve the interests of your students and their topics and units of study.

Book Suggestions

Animals at Risk (Costain 1999)

Bones (Krensky 1999)

Brown Bears (Meadows & Vial 2002) and others in this animal series

Children of the Gold Rush (Murphy & Haigh 2001)—too difficult to read, but the photographs are fun to explore

A Day in the Life of a Police Officer (Hayward 2001)

Fantastic Frogs (Robinson 1999)

How Long Do Animals Live? (Braddock 2000)

Hungry Hungry Sharks (Cole 1986)

Look at Me (McCloskey 1995)

My Life on an Island (James 2001)

Octopus Under the Sea (Roop & Roop 2001)

The Safari Encyclofact (Mondo Publishing, 2000)

Whales and Dolphins (Roop & Roop 2000)

The Zoo (Young 1993)

Publishers of nonfiction series include:

Dominie Press

National Geographic

Newbridge Publishing

Rigby

Safari Books/Mondo Publishing

Sundance Publishing

The Wright Group

■ Challenging Texts and Chapter Books

Ah, the allure of the chapter book, the pinnacle of reading success in the eyes of the beginning reader. Again and again when I interview children, they tell me that they read, or want to read, chapter books. And, why not? They see adults, older siblings, and the classroom's most experienced readers reading Harry Potter, and they want to read it, too.

Kristen Vito says, "First graders love the Henry and Mudge books. They're beginning chapter books. Everybody wants to read them." Cynthia Rylant's wonderful Henry and Mudge series and Arnold Lobel's Frog and Toad books have brought joy and pride to many young readers thirsting for chapter books. Although these series and other early chapter books are considerably above the emergent reading level, they present attainable goals for beginning readers, their language and illustrations inviting young children to "have a go." Although I encourage partners to select books near their level, I also applaud and celebrate their attempts at richer and more challenging texts.

Book Suggestions

Abigail Takes the Wheel (Avi 1999)

The Chalk Box Kid (Bulla 1987)

Days with Frog and Toad (Lobel 1979) and others in this series

Deborah Sampson Goes to War (Stevens 1984)

Gus and Buster Work Things Out (Bronin 1975)

Henry and Mudge series (Rylant)

Cobblestreet Cousins series (Rylant)

■ From the Horse's Mouth: What Kids Say About Books They Love

When talking about the books they love, partners often describe the twists and turns of plot, the surprises, the ahas, and the climaxing moment when once again, all is right with the world. They delight in solving mysteries together: "It's fun in Scooby-Doo, you know, to solve mysteries with my partner. And Scooby and Shaggy are really funny." They discuss and dissect characters for who they are, what they think, and how and why they act.

- "D. W. was jealous because Arthur got to stay home from school, so she colored crayon on her [to simulate chicken pox], but then she got in the tub and it washed off."

- "That giant [in *Rosie's Pool* (Riley 1995)] put suntan lotion all over his face. He was so big and the lotion was so small!"

- "That *Munching Mark* [Cannard 1995], that's all he does, he munches candy."

- "The dog gets mad at the cat 'cause the cat combs the dog from toe to head and the dog looks ree-dick-cue-lous!"

Like readers of all ages, young children love adventures, a hint of danger, a daring rescue: "We like *Clifford and the Big Storm* [Bridwell 1995] 'cause he rescues two boats." They anticipate and predict how stories will turn out, delighting when they are surprised by an unexpected or ironic plot twist. After reading *Video Game* (Prince 1999), a story about a harried mother attempting to rescue her children from the thrall of video games, Tad told me, "The mom says all day, 'Turn off the video,' and then she sneaks down and plays it when the kids are sleeping."

Young children understand and appreciate plot, following story paths wherever they lead, discussing and predicting where the characters and situations will take them: "The mother hippopotamus [in *Mother Hippopotamus' Dry Skin*,

Foundations for Reading, Iversen 2000] gets dry skin and all the other animals tell her to get cream and the elephant tells her to get mud and it works!"

■ Stepping into Books

Losing ourselves in books is one of the greatest pleasures of reading. Living vicariously through the adventures, travails, and triumphs of characters allows us to step outside ourselves and assume new roles through story. We build webs with Wilbur and Charlotte and stand with patient Frog alongside the indomitable Toad, growing gardens and singing to help seeds grow. We imagine we're at a carnival, the smell of popcorn and cotton candy wafting on the breeze. We imagine what life would be like if we were Arthur, running a pet business. Readers make personal connections, living and feeling alongside the characters they love.

■ Revisiting Old Favorites, Chart Stories, and Big Books

Peer partners love to reread favorite stories, books they have practiced and can now read with fluency and expression. In many classrooms I have visited, partners read only books they have read previously in shared or guided reading. In other classrooms, children choose to enjoy old favorites again with partners.

FIG. 8–2 *Environment and modeled writing pieces*

Peer partners can also "read around the room," taking advantage of the text the class has created together—rules, chart stories, poems, and modeled writing. Big books are also favorites with partners, especially those they have read and explored during shared reading. Giving children opportunities to revisit old favorites allows them to focus on fluency, expression, and textual details they may have missed the first time.

■ Libraries and Book Talks

As teachers, we are instrumental in gathering and setting up the classroom library, browsing boxes, and book storage spaces so that partners can find the books they need. Helping children make appropriate selections is a key part of our job. One of the ways many teachers help students, including peer partners, with book selection is by giving book talks. Ideas for book talks are infinite and dictated by the passions of teachers and students. A few suggestions for book talks follow:

1. *Theme collections.* Gather and share books at many levels on a similar theme or topic such as friendship, heroes, sharks, or pets.

2. *A particular genre.* Gather and share books at many levels around a particular genre—poetry books, biographies, mysteries.

3. *Ideas for what to do with books.* Gather and share books at many levels that are used in similar ways—plays, atlases, reference books—and suggest ways readers might share together that diverge from simply opening up a book and reading from cover to cover.

4. *Books you love.* Gather and share books at many levels that you love, or past students have loved, and talk up the qualities that make them special.

5. *Books we love.* Turn the sharing over to your students; have them talk about and swap the books they love best.

I make sure my book talks will appeal to readers at all levels and provide appropriate and interesting choices for every student in the class.

Supporting Peer Partnerships in Progress

9

If you have begun using peer reading partnerships at the start of the year, by midyear you'll be focusing on strengthening and supporting these reading collaborations. Sharon Roberts engages children in literary discussion many times a day. These discussions focus on structure of text, concepts about print, the language and qualities of stories. She models her own reading processes as she reads big books, chart stories, and poems. She "thinks out loud," allowing children to eavesdrop on her literate musings. "In the beginning, it is just modeling. I model, model some more, speak, think aloud, speak, think aloud, and then they internalize the language." As the year progresses, Sharon emphasizes strategies appropriate to emergent readers' development, moving partners from simply using picture clues to "taking a good look at the word," its structure, letter patterns, and meaning.

By midyear, Sharon's first graders speak articulately and wisely about their strategizing. Sharon's modeling has been powerful and pervasive, and children not only reiterate and replicate her teaching but also apply strategies with confidence and creativity:

- "Well, there's three ways I help my partner. Sound out the word, look for a vowel, or see if there's a cluster. And don't forget to think—to see what makes sense."

- "Partners can help you with silent *es*. Sometimes you don't hear an *e* and you think it's not there, but your partner catches it."

FIG. 9–1

- "They can give a hint. If it's starting with their name, and you didn't know that, they could say, 'This starts with my name' and if you still don't get it, they give you a better hint."

It is early March in Kristen Vito's first grade. As students trickle in at the start of the day, stowing backpacks, then greeting their friends and teachers, Kristen sits at a large horseshoe table under the windows at the far end of the room. Students check in with her, then say hello to Stephanie, the student teacher, before beginning the work of the day. Most children choose to read or write. Some are writing stories; others are doing research for informational pieces. Still others are reading alone or with a partner. As Kristen confers with her student teacher, her eyes scan the room. Occasionally, she interrupts her conversation with Stephanie to ask a child or pair of children if they are making good choices.

Nine students have elected to read with partners. One pair, Lynn and Fiona, sit in a large white rocking chair, each holding her own copy of *If You Give a Mouse a Cookie* (Numeroff 1985):

Lynn
So you'll read to him
from one of

and he'll ask

Fiona
So you'll read to him

your books
and he'll ask
to see [pauses on *pictures*]

[Points to *pictures,* runs her hand
over the page to indicate that what they
are looking at is a picture] *p–p–puh*

picture . . . pictures.

Lynn and Fiona continue choral reading, assisting each other, responsibility for reading shifting word by word, phrase by phrase. As they complete a book, they rise to select another. When this happens, another reading pair, Jane and Anna, jump up from the rug to take their place in the rocking chair. This seat switching between these two pairs of readers happens four times during the forty-five-minute reading period. Each time a partnership goes in search of a new book, the other hops up to sit in the rocker. Once seated, partners resume reading immediately.

Across the room, Rob and Carl sit side by side on a soft leather couch, each holding a copy of *Henry and Mudge and the Starry Night* (Rylant 1998). Nat sits beside them holding a different title in the Henry and Mudge series. While Rob and Carl read chorally, Nat sometimes reads his own book and sometimes follows along with their reading. Throughout the reading, Rob uses his finger to keep his place, to aid in blending sounds of unfamiliar words, and to stay focused. Carl uses his finger occasionally when decoding words or finding his place. These partners read in unison, each assuming the lead at times, each contributing when he is able. In the interchange below, the text they are reading is: "It was a beautiful night. Henry and Henry's parents lay on their backs by the fire and looked at the sky."

Rob	Carl
It was	
	It was
a beautiful night	
	a beautiful night
Henry and Henry's	*Henry's*
parents lay on their backs	
	on their backs
by the fire and	
[Pauses on *looked*]	
	looked at the sky.
looked at the sky.	

Although Rob leads this particular segment of the reading, at other times Carl leads and Rob echoes, and sometimes they read in unison. Each reader is focused and involved, their enjoyment of and interest in the adventures of Henry and Mudge evident in the conversations that precede and follow this reading segment.

At this point in the year, partner reading is a choice Kristen's students can make as needed when reading independently. Kristen says, "At times, I find certain text selections, like Henry and Mudge, are really popular and children are so motivated. So two guys want to get together and tackle that book. Choosing to read together is all about interests or friendships." Clearly, Rob and Carl choose to read together out of a mutual interest in this particular story as well as their friendship. When watching these readers I ask myself, as I do often when observing partners, whether a challenging text like this might have defeated each one had he chosen to read it alone.

Many of Kristen's students speak of friendship when talking about peer partnerships: "It's more funner and more easier when you're with a friend; when you're alone it's really quiet." Other children say they like to read with people who share interests or read at the same level: "I like meeting new friends and finding a just-right friend for me—you know, someone who reads like you do, the same kind of books." And many children mention how they appreciate a partner's assistance, especially with word solving: "If I don't know a word, I ask them and they tell me." Still other students prefer to read alone because "it's peaceful and quiet, I can concentrate" or "there's no one talking to you."

Kristen believes that peer reading partnerships "establish a community of learners—a family culture—and they forge relationships between children. They get relationships going and set the foundations for literature discussion groups." Literature discussions between pairs of readers "help children be collaborative, supportive partners in thought."

After many months of learning about, modeling, discussing, and practicing partnerships, Kristen's students have developed into self-directed, focused learners, well aware of what constitute "good choices." Throughout the day, Kristen guides and observes, stressing always the importance of "making good choices." She models and instructs, then steps back, respecting children's choices and trusting them to find reading situations and structures that work for them.

■ The Importance of Choice

Reading with a partner is a choice students make in many classrooms. Allowing choice ensures that readers who benefit from reading partnerships will have frequent opportunities to engage in such constructive reading. Choosing to read with a partner is only one of many choices associated with peer partnerships. Other choices include:

- who will partner with whom

- where partners will sit

- what books they will read

- what kinds of strategies they will use to help and support each other

- what kinds of conversations they will have before, during, and after reading

- what kinds of extension activities to undertake

Kristen models and gives children frequent reminders about making good choices, supporting peer partnerships in many ways:

> I model with my assistant, I model with my student teacher, I call a child up and we try something together. Again, it's lots of positive reinforcement. I walk around when I'm not modeling, highlighting everyone who is making very good choices, who is being constructive and using the time wisely. I really respond to good choices.
>
> I've experimented through the years. There were years when I did the ear-to-ear, back-to-back routine. I finally abandoned that; I find it so artificial. When in your life as a reader would you be doing that? Never. So now it's much more casual, more real-life situations. I stress side by side. There are lots of comfortable spots in the room, like the couch, and we have lamps that are lit. One of my students has a parent who sews, so I have ten pillows around the room. I try to have readers go to a comfortable spot. They know they have to use five-inch voices. They know they have to try to maintain the task and be focused on reading. Then, they know that I expect them to talk about the book. They know that ultimately there is going to be that responsibility—to report back, talk about what they have done.

Kristen's main goal is "building a community of literate people" and her students go about their reading work with confidence and industry, helping each other when necessary, choosing to work alone or together as interests, passions, and needs dictate. By midyear, many of her first graders' reading is fluent, and their focus is centered on meaning. Kristen says, "They will use the cueing systems to help each other, but there is always the issue of fluency and maintaining the flow of the story."

Many students indicate that they prefer to read books chorally with their partner. Research suggests that choral reading may, indeed, be young readers' preferred means of maintaining fluency and sense of story (Griffin 2000), especially after partnerships are well established and pairs of students are collaborating effectively. When reading chorally, partners more easily retain the rhythm and flow of story through their joint construction of text. Students' overwhelming preference for choral reading over other ways of taking turns, such as alternating pages, suggests the importance they place on fluency and meaning.

■ Assistive Behavior

At midyear, we want to continue providing time for children to share and discuss effective assistive strategies. We also want to ask them to model what works for them. Most teachers expect partners to use cueing systems, but they are also aware of the importance of fluency and not interrupting the flow of stories. Kristen stresses "pacing yourself and your partner, helping each other keep up." When Kristen models the importance of attending to punctuation when reading, she'll then often observe children coaching one another about using punctuation. They'll also mention attending to punctuation when asked how they assist one another.

■ Pairing Considerations

Within literate communities, children appreciate the autonomy to choose whether to pair with someone. They also value their "partners in thought." Sharon Roberts says that she sees value in many types of partnerships. Often her nurturing students work well with less secure children, patiently supporting their reading, but she wonders if these relationships are the best partnerships for these readers. "As the year goes on, I design more flexible partnerships, sometimes based on children's social needs, sometimes on their development, sometimes on their interests."

All teachers need to decide for themselves what pairing system or strategy best suits the needs of their students and their program. At midyear, teachers may decide to:

- Continue pairing students with partners of approximately equal expertise.

- Allow students to choose a partner from their guided reading group.

- Occasionally let students choose a partner from among the entire class. This works particularly well in classrooms where children are experienced and reading well independently.

If I have paired children of approximately equal expertise, challenges at midyear may still revolve around level: depending on the text selected, reader interest and background play important roles in determining expertise and ability.

FIG. 9–2

Usually readers at similar levels negotiate these differences, supporting each other in texts as they are able. When social or emotional factors also come into play, collaboration often becomes trickier. Some readers are too vulnerable and self-conscious to feel comfortable reading with a partner. Pairing them with a "nurturing buddy" may help, but no matter how caring the partner, some children refuse to engage.

Readers reluctant to read with only one other person may feel more comfortable in a small group, the larger number of participants taking off some of the pressure. For those readers, buddy circles might make more sense, at least initially, until they gain more confidence. Other readers, no matter what the conditions or structures, cannot seem to relax and participate in partner reading effectively.

■ Challenges for Partnerships in Progress

Peer partnerships are supported and strengthened in classrooms in which there is a sustained and purposeful focus on reading as a fluent, meaning-making process. Challenges in using partnerships center around:

- encouraging children's collaborative and assistive skills and strategies

- helping hesitant readers find more meaningful ways to read

- helping readers talk about books and discuss what makes good literature

- pairing children with peers who have passions they can share

As Kristen says, "Kids are much better salesmen than I am" when it comes to recommending books to each other.

When I interview students and ask them what is hard about working with a partner, their responses center mostly on the process of reading or on classroom distractions:

- "Staying together. It's hard to keep together—they read faster than me."

- "They tell me the word. I want to do it."

- "Sometimes the words are hard. We can't get 'em."

- "Sometimes it's too loud and sometimes we talk a lot."

- "Reading all together. Some of us can't catch up."

- "When you get stuck on a word and they say, 'No, it's this word or that word!'"

When I observe partnerships struggling with collaboration or process, I take several steps. First, I sit alongside, listening. Sometimes, this is enough to encourage friendlier, more cooperative behavior. If not, I make suggestions or redirect. If I notice several partnerships struggling with similar issues, I plan and facilitate minilessons to suggest alternative ways of sharing books. Following are a few ideas.

- If partners cannot stay together reading chorally, I suggest or model reading alternate pages.

- If partners are "nagging" readers or shouting instructions, I remind them about kind words and "friendly ways" to help the reader and/or ask for student volunteers to model such behavior.

- If listeners always tell the word when a reader pauses, I encourage them to wait a little, allowing the reader to think, sometimes even suggesting a way to make waiting easier, such as "count to ten" or "take three deep breaths."

- If hinting is slowing reading to the point where understanding is compromised, I sometimes suggest that the listening partner tell the word.

- If one partner has taken over and is doing most of the reading, I ask two successful collaborators to demonstrate for the group how they share reading and take turns. After the demonstration, we discuss and highlight *each* partner's contribution.

- If partners' book selections seem inappropriate, I browse the library with them, helping them choose books at their level. If this is a persistent problem, I request that partners show me the books they select beforehand.

- If partners are experiencing friction, I sit in as coach, encouraging and suggesting positive behavior. If the problem persists, I split them up.

- If readers have difficulty working in one-on-one partnerships, I introduce buddy circles in which they can read with a small group of readers at their level.

- If a child truly cannot work with others, I allow him to read alone, usually books at his guided reading level.

I do not require fluent or more experienced readers to read aloud with partners. Instead I provide them with alternative ways to collaborate following their silent reading of text. (See Chapter 10 for partner ideas for fluent readers.)

Teachers best know their students—their interests, social alliances, and academic needs. As they listen to and observe students reading in partnership, they make informed decisions about the kinds of instruction readers need to move forward. As is true for any instructional strategy, peer partnerships do not always run smoothly, and children do not always cooperate or collaborate in ways that further their reading development. It is at such times that teachers must step in to offer support and guidance.

◼ Summing Up

Once peer reading partnerships have been established, we want to model constructive assistive behavior and give children many opportunities to share their growing expertise with others. We also want to make sure children are paired with compatible partners so that these interactions support their development as readers. Although each teacher will have particular goals and considerations in planning and structuring peer partner reading, recommendations for midyear include:

- Continue to create strategy charts with children, post these "how to help my partner" and "rules for partners" prominently and refer to them often.

- Provide many opportunities for partners to share and discuss effective strategies and model them for their peers.

- Consider including comprehension-building activities such as retelling, summarizing, drawing conclusions, and writing responses to their reading.

Environment, time, and space considerations matter. How students and teachers organize reading partnerships matters, and artful pairing does make a difference. In the end, however, it is our trust in children and our ability to truly listen and respond that make the difference for peer partnerships and all aspects of our literacy programs. Taking the time to listen and support young readers and creating a nurturing environment for their collaborative reading relationships are well worth it! As first-grader Allen says, "It's a great friend to have when you're reading with a buddy. I think everyone in the world should have one."

Adapting the Model: Peer Partnerships for All Students

10

No matter how we adapt or change the model, it is important to involve all students in collaborative reading. Access to the thinking of others helps individuals build knowledge, something we want for all our learners. Peer partnerships can be adapted to meet the needs of:

- inclusion classrooms and readers with special needs

- classrooms in which readers' first language is not English

- classrooms in which some readers are already fluent

■ Supporting Readers with Special Needs

Midyear in Gia Renaud's first grade, Kevin, Angel, and Nina sit on the carpet in a row, Kevin in the middle. Kevin is reading, the others helping as needed. After his book is completed, it is Angel's turn; the group switches places so that Angel is now in the middle. This scenario is repeated many times as the three children take turns reading. When allowed to make decisions about their learning preferences in an environment with clear, specific expectations about responsible, cooperative behavior, children create organizational structures that work for them. There is nothing on the classroom buddy reading chart about this switching seats or taking turns, but Kevin, Angel, and Nina have devised a structure that allows every member to participate.

FIG. 10–1 *Me and my best friend*

Gia has just started pairing children for reading. She hopes partner reading will give readers practice and exposure to books while building fluency. "Even for my nonreaders, it gets them working together. They read together and it gets them listening to each other. Some children can't quite get the idea of hinting, but they enjoy the time anyway, just being together."

Six of Gia's students have individual education programs, one is autistic and has a full-time aide, and another is severely handicapped by cerebral palsy. In addition to the full-time aide, Gia is assisted by a building reading specialist. A number of her children receive special services throughout the day. I interviewed eight of Gia's students, all of whom preferred reading with a partner to reading alone. Their comments illustrate the social and academic importance these readers put on these collaborative relationships: "I like reading with a partner 'cause I'm not very good at reading, and you can get help." Their remarks also speak to their perceptions about the sometimes overwhelming task of reading, and the appreciation of their partner's support: "I read one page, and he can read one page. Nobody has to read the whole thing." Finally, Gia's students describe how they enjoy collaborating to create meaning and stories together: "We take turns. I usually help him and we have a very good story."

Learning from Gia and Her Students

Gia's classroom offers a number of challenges related to children's behavior and learning difficulties. Although she tries to pair readers of approximately equal expertise, she must also pair readers with nonreaders if everyone is to participate. Most times, the autistic child listens to stories read by his aide during partner reading. Occasionally, a classmate will also read to him. Mark, the child with cerebral palsy, is also a nonreader, so he sits with another partnership, listening as they read and discuss books. Many of Gia's students talk about how they like to read to the nonreaders. Phil says, "Some people read very good. I don't, but I help Mark." Timmy says, "My favorite partner is Albie [the autistic child] because, well, I like him and I like to read to him. I help him."

Although students enjoy reading with a partner, they also acknowledge the challenges of collaboration. As Timmy says, "Sometimes they get me affused [confused]. It's really hard to read, and Angel tells me. Words are hard if you don't know 'em."

When she begins partner reading, Gia and her students make a chart, which is posted on the wall:

How to Be a Good Reading Partner

1. Help your reading partner.
2. Take turns.
3. Sit next to your partner.
4. Listen to your partner.

Gia refers to this, reminding children of their thoughts and ideas, every day before they begin reading. There is also a chart outlining strategies when "you come to a word you don't know":

1. Look at the first letter (*d*ay).
2. Look for a little word in the big word (*to*–day).

3. Skip it and read the rest of the sentence. Then go back.

4. Look at the picture clue [picture of a sun and the word *sun*].

5. Ask a friend.

Gia encourages partners to think of these strategies when helping each other.

Gia's students' literate conversations reveal their understanding of the complexities and challenges of reading:

- "He helps me find a chunk."

- "We skip and see what makes sense."

- "We look at the pictures, then the words."

- "When I'm stuck, he tells me what to do, like look at the pictures, look for the word inside."

- "He tracks along and he makes sure I don't make a mistake."

Gia's students demonstrate that peers come in many guises and that even self-conscious readers derive pleasure, satisfaction, and confidence from sitting with and reading to others. She has found a way to adapt and modify partnership reading so that it works for her students. Is it worth it? Listen to Missy: "I go to Reading Recovery. My partner does, too. If we have the same books, we read the same pages. You're having lots of fun with them and stuff. If we're stuck, she helps me. I help, too, and, like, we don't tell the word and stuff."

Suggestions for Adapting Peer Partnerships in Inclusion Classrooms

Inclusion classrooms present unique challenges for implementing peer partnerships for reading. Particularly challenging is pairing readers of approximately equal expertise. To accomplish this in most inclusion settings would mean leaving children out. To involve all students, even nonreaders, teachers make special adaptations that allow all students to participate. Instead of peer-to-peer partnerships, variations in pairing include:

- An adult with a child (for disabled or younger reader).

- A more experienced student reader with a less experienced, emergent reader.

Activities for these partners might include, but are not limited to the following.

1. *Taped books.* An experienced reader and an emergent reader pair to listen to a taped story, then discuss it.

2. *Rereading favorite books.* An experienced reader and an emergent reader "re-read" a very familiar big book or story.

3. *Echo reading.* The experienced reader reads a line, then the emergent reader "echoes" this same line.

4. *Paired reading* (Topping 1987, 1989). The experienced reader supports the efforts of the emergent reader. A form of cross-ability pairing, paired reading was originally designed for parents and children but can also be used effectively in the classroom with readers in grades K–5:

   - The emergent reader selects reading materials at her instructional level.
   - Paired readers then find a comfortable reading spot.
   - Before reading, partners establish silent signals to indicate when the emergent reader wants to read solo and when she is tired and needs a break. In the latter instance, the experienced reader takes over, reading for a short time until her partner once again joins her.
   - Readers begin reading chorally.
   - If the emergent reader miscues then corrects herself on her own, her partner offers praise. When the emergent reader miscues, her partner waits five seconds, then tells the word. (Student-to-student paired readers can be told to count to five before supplying the word.) Partners then begin reading chorally until the emergent reader once again signals that she wants to read solo.
   - At the end of a session, partners talk about reading and "how it went."
   - The pair might also discuss difficult words in the text or interesting segments, centering their thoughts on meaning.

Topping (1989) suggests that paired reading be done at least three times a week for a minimum of six weeks, each session lasting between fifteen and thirty minutes. However, many variations are possible if you are using paired reading as a fluency strategy. The Bureau of Education and Research publishes two short training videos (Burrill & Paulsen 1998) that clearly explain steps and procedures for paired reading.

■ Supporting English Language Learners

Christine Wiltshire gathers her students on the carpet to preview and discuss a book titled *We Need Dentists* (Schafer 2000), which she plans to read to them later in the day. She tells the children they need to "activate their brains," then leads a five-minute discussion about the book, eliciting what they know about dentists and what dentists do. As the children share ideas, Christine flips to pages of the book that illustrate the concepts students are discussing. Finally, she sets the book aside, telling them she will read it later but that they are free to read or look through it during partner reading.

Christine's quick discussion calls up children's prior knowledge about dentists and clues in those children who aren't familiar with dentists. For her English language learners, Christine introduces language and conceptual terms, then links them to illustrations in the text. Christine's discussion ensures that *all* her first graders will come to the read-aloud of *We Need Dentists* with background, concepts, and language that will help them understand it.

Christine's fellow first-grade teacher, Sarah Rich, begins reading workshop by leading her first graders in a spirited retelling of *The Snowy Day* (Keats 1962). As they retell, Sarah holds up question/picture cards that prompt them to recall events in the story. The cards, which ask questions such as who, what, when, and where, help students focus on important details. When the retelling is complete, Sarah reviews the day's reading workshop activity: children will reread *The Snowy Day* with a partner, then prepare and revise their own "snowy day booklet" (an abbreviated retelling of the story that includes their own illustrations) and read it to their partner.

The Snowy Day is an excellent text for all beginning readers, especially students learning English as their second language, because the match between print and illustrations beautifully supports the emergent reader. Sarah's simply constructed prompts are effective in encouraging *all* students' participation. This is especially important for English language learners. Participating in the supported retelling gives children resources on which to draw in rereading the book with their partner and completing their individual retellings of this challenging text. Visual prompts, especially when they include both text and illustrations, bring all students more fully into the conversation.

Suggestions for English Language Learners

Like all learners, students learning English as a second language need explicit teaching, clear modeling, and many demonstrations of strategies for reading alone and in partnership. They also need opportunities for guided and independent practice if they are to make strategies and skills their own. In addition to the best practices embedded in most comprehensive literacy programs, English language learners benefit from repetition of lessons and strategy demonstrations given to the whole class. These enhanced learning and teaching experiences should focus explicitly on vocabulary development and include both auditory and visual presentations. English language learners also need many opportunities to hear written language through teacher read-alouds and shared reading activities so that they internalize the sounds and rhythms of print.

As young children work to acquire speaking and reading facility in a second language, talk and interaction are critical. English language learners also need many and varied opportunities to engage in real reading and writing. Although talking about books and strategies benefits all young readers, it is especially critical for children struggling to master a new language. Talk during authentic literacy activities like peer partnerships certainly benefits English language learners.

There are also many other ways teachers can ensure that English language learners more fully participate in all reading-related endeavors. A few things to keep in mind when implementing partnerships for English language learners would be:

- Reteach lessons and strategies taught to the whole class.

- Encourage partner talk about all aspects of text—illustrations, print, and of course meaning.

- Provide many opportunities for English language learners to hear written text read aloud, especially the kinds of text they may then read with a partner.

- Offer extra "book talks" and book introductions geared to English language learners' background knowledge before partner reading.

- Preteach vocabulary and text patterns students will encounter in partner reading.

- Present lessons for partners using both visual and auditory cues.

■ Adapting Partnerships for Fluent Readers

"I like to read alone more than I like to read with a partner, because it's peaceful." Many fluent readers have made the transition into mature silent reading and therefore prefer to read alone. All readers benefit from reading aloud occasionally, especially with texts such as poems and plays that are meant to be spoken. Reading aloud strengthens fluency and allows readers to hear and appreciate the language of written text. However, asking fluent readers to read independent reading books aloud on a regular basis is developmentally inappropriate. Reading aloud slows reading and encourages word-by-word reading and "word calling" (saying the words in one's head), difficult habits to break later on. For young fluent readers, there is still value in reading collaboration, but activities and strategies should now focus on interactions before, while, and after each individual reads the text on her or his own.

As the year progresses and children are able to read such books as Lobel's Frog and Toad series or Rylant's Henry and Mudge books fluently, teachers may cut back on peer partnerships and encourage children to read silently on their own. Or partners may continue to sit shoulder to shoulder, silently reading their own copy of the same book, pausing at times to share and discuss their reading. As Sharon Roberts says, "My primary expectation is that they are engaged with their partner and engaged with a piece of literature." Whether this happens as part of shared oral reading or a discussion or other shared activity following silent reading depends on the reading level and development of the readers involved. If, like Kristen Vito, we expect peer partnerships to "set the foundation for literature discussion groups" and help students to be "collaborative, supportive partners in thought," then we will want to plan ways to extend these collaborative reading relationships beyond joint oral reading.

Suggestions for Fluent Readers

A few suggestions for text-related activities follow, but you should develop strategies that suit the needs of your fluent readers and your curriculum.

- *Semantic maps.* During or after reading, partners complete story maps or nonfiction graphic organizers. (See Appendices H through M for maps, charts, and nonfiction organizers.) There are many resources for such organizers such as Bromley (1991) and Witherell and McMackin (2002).

- *Character studies.* After reading a story, partners can reread it, this time assuming the role of a character or characters. They can also:
  - complete a "character map" like those found in Appendix H, I, or J to help them get into their character's head
  - write a letter to their favorite character

- plan and write a new adventure for a character with their partner, then share it with the class

- *Reading responses.* Partners respond to reading in variety of ways through talk and writing. Have them use questions like these to trigger thoughts about characters, style, setting, mood, theme, and plot.

  - *Characters.* Do any of the characters remind you of yourself or anyone you know? How would you describe the main character if you were telling a friend about her?
  - *Setting.* Where does the story take place? How does this setting impact the story?
  - *Style.* What special words or expressions does the author use to help you *see* the story?
  - *Mood.* What part of the story makes you feel happy, sad, scared, or excited?
  - *Theme.* What is the author telling you? What is the story's message?
  - *Plot.* What events happened in the story? What was the biggest event? What caused this event? What happened as a result of this event?

- *Roles for literature sharing.* As they do in literature circles, partners can assume specific roles related to stories and text, taking responsibility for reporting after reading. These roles include:

  - predictor (predicts before and during reading)
  - summarizer (summarizes during or after reading)
  - wordsmith (finds interesting words to define and share)
  - illustrator (illustrates an important or favorite part)
  - "passage-smith" (finds interesting and meaningful phrases to read and share)

- *Rereading for expression.* Partners choose a favorite passage, read, reread, and practice reading with meaning as the author intended.

- *Found poems* (Edinger 2000). These poems can be "found" in any text that resonates for readers. When I introduce this activity, I model by reading a favorite snippet (usually a page or two) of evocative text with lots of expression. I then go back and reread, selecting powerful words and phrases to write down in stanza form, creating a found poem. Fluent readers can create found poems together or individually, then share them with the class.

Partners in Thinking

Draw and write about what you and your partner were thinking and doing while reading together.

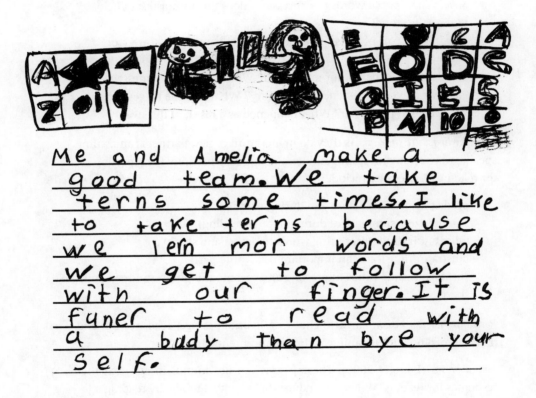

Me and Amelia make a
good team. We take
terns some times. I like
to take terns because
we lern mor words and
we get to follow
with our finger. It is
funer to read with
a budy than bye your
self.

FIG. 10–2 *Terry's thinking*

Children (and even college students!) typically love creating found poems and are delighted and amazed by the powerful text they create.

- *Book talks*. Partners read different books, then give a book talk to their partners. In preparing for their book talks, readers ask:

  - What can I tell about the characters?
  - What illustrations or passages could I share to "hook" the reader?
  - What aspects of the plot do I want to share?
  - Can I make connections to this book and others my partner knows?
  - What can I tell about setting, tone, mood, or author's style that will interest my partner?

■ Summing Up

As educators, we must always remember to take our cues *from students*. Each class and each partnership is unique, and we want to give *all* children opportunities to grow and develop their own strategies and structures for peer partnerships within the goals we, as teachers, have set for them. Learning communities are created and sustained by the joint pursuits of individual members. If we choose to use a reading strategy like peer partnerships, we want to make certain that we plan and adapt the model so that all learners can participate and enjoy the benefits and pleasures of literate collaboration.

Strategy Bookmark Templates 1

Ways to help my partner	Choosing just-right books

Strategy Bookmark Templates 2

Rules for partners	What do we do when we don't know a word?

Literacy Minilessons

Minilessons on Processes

- reading from left to right
- matching print word by word
- pointing to keep place
- reading in different ways
  - reading the pictures
  - using the words
- using strategies to solve unfamiliar words
- reading in "chunks"/using appropriate phrasing
- paying attention to pace—not too slow, not too fast
- reading with expression
- reading "as the author intended"
- keeping the focus on meaning
  - predicting
  - inferring
  - drawing conclusions
  - thinking aloud
- asking questions while reading

Minilessons on Procedures

- using the classroom library, book bins, bookmarks, leveled collections
- choosing just-right books
- reading "within one's space" (using a quiet voice)
- asking for help from teacher or peers
- using the table of contents
- using the index and glossary

Minilessons on Skills

- developing decoding skills
- using letter–sound knowledge
- recognizing letter and word patterns
- learning phonetic rules and generalizations
- learning about contractions, compound words, homonyms, and so on.
- blending and decoding "long and short words"

Minilessons on Qualities and Conventions

- hearing and understanding an author's voice and style
- recognizing and understanding text structures
  - cause and effect
  - compare and contrast
  - chronological order/time sequence
- using punctuation to make meaning
- using text "signals"
  - bold print
  - italicized print
  - capitalized print

Minilessons to Support and Enhance Effective Partnering

- hinting, not telling
- taking a deep breath (or counting silently to five) before jumping in to help
- developing rules for partners
- sitting beside one's partner
- sharing a book/taking turns
- having literate conversations/talking about books
- talking about characters
- talking about plot
- talking about setting and why it is important
- retelling a story
- using partner reading voices
- finding just-right books
- "tasting" a book (reading cover, opening pages, and so on) to see if it is right for both partners
- helping a partner with nonverbal cues (for example, pointing)
- using tools
- getting organized/making decisions
- reading different kinds of books (fiction, nonfiction, poetry, song books, and so on)
- fixing the partnership
- recognizing and using supportive talk

Partner Names _____ _____ Date _____

Partners in Thinking

Draw and write about what you and your partner were thinking and doing while reading together.

_____

_____

_____

_____

_____

_____

_____

_____

_____

Names _____ Date _____

What Is It About Partners?

Draw and write about why you like working with partners or "buddy" groups.

_____

_____

_____

_____

_____

_____

_____

_____

_____

Partner Names _____   _____ Date _____

Rules for Partners

Make a list of important things for partners to remember when reading together.

Partner Names _____ _____ Date _____

Character Map

Draw and write about a story character.

Where does he/she live?

What does he/she look like?

What does he/she do?

What does he/she say?

Character's Name

What is her/his problem?

What feelings does he/she have?

How does the problem get solved?

Partner Names _____ _____ Date _____

Comparing Characters

Choose two characters and compare how they are alike and different.

Character 1   Character 2

Things in Common

Partner Names _____   _____ Date _____

Comparing Characters

Choose two characters and compare how they are alike and different.

Character 1   Character 2

Things in Common

Partner Names _____ _____ Date _____

Story Circle

Draw and tell the story. Be sure to mark the beginning and end.

Partner Names _____ _____ Date _____

Web of Information

Draw and write about your topic. Start your web in the middle and branch out! Be sure to add extra branches as needed.

Your Topic

Partner Names _____ _____ Date _____

K—W—L

Draw and write about what you and your partner KNOW, WANT TO KNOW, and LEARNED from your reading.

K	W	L
What we *know*	What we *want to know*	What we *learned*

Classroom Research: Teachers/Literacy Programs

Teachers: Christine Wiltshire and Sarah Rich
Grade Level: Grade 1
Number of Students: 15 (some ELL) in each classroom

School Description: Christine and Sarah teach in a K–4 urban charter school with a curriculum centering on maritime studies. The student population reflects the demographics of the large northeastern city in which it is situated, and students come from many cultures and backgrounds.

Program Description: Both classrooms have literature-based reading programs using little books and guided reading. Routines include teacher read-alouds, shared reading, guided reading, centers (listening, poetry, writing, and ABC centers), and at least one half hour of sustained silent reading. Sarah does lots of genre exploration. Both teachers encourage children to select just-right books. Classroom walls are covered with print—word walls and posters as well as charts and poems created with the children. Students and teachers add words to word walls daily, and children write and practice word wall words. Daily minilessons introduce and reinforce reading skills and strategies children use during whole-class work, guided reading, independent reading, and buddy reading. Writing workshop happens every day.

Students also write in journals and during center time. By midyear, Christine and Sarah are supporting writers through all phases of the writing process: writing, revising, editing, and publishing. In both classrooms, writing workshop begins with a minilesson, then children write for extended periods. Time is always allotted for sharing at the close of writing workshop. Children's writing is also incorporated into the "Person of the Week" (Christine's room) and "Student of the Week" (Sarah's room) bulletin boards, which use writing, pictures, and photographs to highlight a different student each week. Finally, students participate in shared and interactive writing, creating songs, poems, and stories that are displayed on classroom walls.

Both Christine and Sarah integrate word study into all literacy activities. Children learn and practice word-solving skills and strategies through daily minilessons and activities at the ABC center. They learn and practice word solving through shared reading and interactive writing. Students participate in "making words" activities (Cunningham & Hall 1994), they read and write poems and rhymes, and they play word-solving games. Both classrooms have individualized spelling programs—children progress through a "first-grade list" of words at their own pace. Each week individuals select the words they will learn. After consultation with the teacher, these words are placed in spelling notebooks and practiced and learned at home and at school.

Teacher: Kristen Vito
Grade Level: Grade 1
Number of Students: 23

School Description: Kristen teaches in a public school, a K–1 early learning center located in a suburb adjacent to a large northeastern city. Three days a week, Kristen has the support of a resource teacher for part of the day. She also has a student teacher every semester and uses many parent volunteers to assist in the classroom. Kristen says, "I tend to get interesting kids, many with occupational therapy issues, visual perception difficulties, and other learning needs. This is often the last stop for some children, but no matter what conditions you start with, they rise to the occasion." All of her students this particular year come from homes in which English is the first language.

Program Description: Kristen's students follow an individualized reading program. She tells me, "I do not do guided reading." Rather, her students follow their own passions, reading individually or with partners. The heart of Kristen's reading program is the independent reading children engage in every day. Students select books from a large classroom library—stories, nonfiction, and poetry. They read classmates' writing as well as other written materials available throughout the room. Within the structure of independent reading, children sometimes read alone and sometimes with partners. During independent reading, Kristen and her fellow teachers check in, conferring and monitoring children's activities. Kristen says that this gives them an opportunity to "highlight positive, responsible behavior" and remind children about "good and appropriate literate choices."

Kristen and her colleagues use many models of reading. Teachers read aloud picture books and novels. Shared reading of charts, poems, big books, and text on projected transparencies allows teachers to model all kinds of reading and writing strategies. Kristen and her colleagues begin the year with "lots of shared reading," tapering off as the year progresses and children become fluent readers. Through teacher read-alouds, shared reading, and independent reading, Kristen's students encounter a variety of genres. She explains, "Genres are introduced through reading, then expanded to include students' writing." In all that she does, Kristen seeks to build a community of learners, "helping children lead literate lives." Literature discussion groups are a critical facet of her reading program. Groups meet during and after teacher read-alouds and shared reading and also after students' independent reading, when Kristen asks readers to share something about their book.

Kristen has a comprehensive writing program closely tied to students' reading. Their reading responses extend and expand on literature discussions. Students also write in a variety of genres: narratives, descriptive pieces, letters, and informational writing, this last "especially tied to their reading of nonfiction." Children write for distinct purposes with specific goals in mind. For example, a previous year's class wrote letters to local furniture stores saying they needed comfortable seating for reading. This campaign resulted in the donation of three large and comfortable leather couches, one of which sits in Kristen's room; the other two reside in other classrooms.

Until December, Kristen asks students to "freewrite." Once they are fluent, she begins to take them through the entire writing process as they work through drafts, or "sloppy copies"; edits and revisions; and finally, "published pieces." Because published pieces are handwritten by the students, Kristen collaborates with the school's occupational therapist to "make children's handwriting smooth, easy, and legible."

During shared reading, Kristen models many word-solving strategies on chart paper, the blackboard, and projected transparencies. She does not do a weekly spelling list and is "not crazy about word walls; I don't see them being used in the spirit in which they were designed." Instead, she wants her students to have more immediate, hands-on access to words, which she accomplishes with sheets of commonly used words that she gives to each child. The second half of the year, Kristen targets three words a week that she wants them to work with at centers and in their writing. In addition to checking children's writing every day, she also administers a developmental spelling list once a quarter to monitor children's progress. During the second half of the year, she expects students to know these commonly used words. Students must use the sheets to "fix their writing. I say, 'Here's the list, go back and circle the words that you really think you did not spell correctly.' The lists are in alphabetical order so children find the word and fix it, then write it. I'm stressing strategies that are real life. When I don't know a word, I go to the dictionary, I use alphabetical order. So I'm trying to reinforce that a little more, trying always to make connections between the known and the unknown: if you can do this, you can do that."

Teacher: Sharon Roberts
Grade Level: Grade 1
Number of Students: 20

School Description: Sharon teaches in a large suburban elementary school. All of her students come from homes in which English is the first language.

Program Description: Sharon characterizes her reading program as "a mix between shared reading and our core reading program. It's a combination in which children are exposed to the same core literature and then I pull groups at children's instructional level for guided reading." All grades, K–3, in Sharon's school use a commercial reading series as the core of their literacy program. Sharon teaches an anthology story for shared reading early in the week. Children then reread this story with partners later in the week for practice and to build fluency and comprehension. Sharon also reads aloud to the children several times a day from a wide variety of picture books, both fiction and nonfiction.

Sharon assesses students regularly using running records and the district-required reading assessment. She then groups children by level for guided reading, selecting from a wide variety of little books housed in the school's recently created "literacy closet." Guided reading groups change often according to children's development and interests. For guided reading, Sharon tends to use a lot of nonfiction. "They love it, and many of my kids say at the end of the year that they like to read nonfiction more than fiction."

Students write regularly in journals and during writing workshop, experimenting with many types of writing throughout the year: narrative, persuasive, descriptive, informational, poetry, letters. Children create story maps and write retellings and responses to reading. They also write across the curriculum in math, science, and social studies.

Sharon follows a sequential program of word study that builds children's awareness of the alphabetic nature of written language and strengthens their word-solving skills and strategies. This word study program includes regular focused minilessons, a spelling program, and many chances for children to practice and refine skills and strategies in context. In everything she does, Sharon consciously endeavors to build children's language about reading strategies, encouraging them to articulate their thinking to themselves and others. This is reflected in the way children talk about reading and strategizing with their partners.

Teacher: Joy Richardson
Grade Level: Grade 1
Number of Students: 17

School Description: Joy teaches in a large regional elementary school.

Program Description: Joy's reading program is literature based, with guided reading as its instructional grounding. The district supports a commercial reading series, encouraging teachers to use the anthology stories for shared reading while making time every day for guided reading at students' instructional reading level. For the past three years, Joy's school has been involved with the federal Reading Excellence grant program. As part of this initiative, a literacy coach provides twice monthly inservice, and grant monies have been used to create an extensive collection of over five hundred sets of leveled reading books for guided reading.

Joy reads one or two picture books aloud to her students every day. Her children often write responses to teacher read-alouds, making personal and text-to-text connections. Joy also uses one or two anthology stories a month for shared reading, choosing ones children will enjoy. Children may sometimes pair up to practice the selection several more times, or complete a related activity in pairs or alone. Joy also shares big books, chart stories, poems, and V.I.P. charts with her class. V.I.P. charts highlight a different child each week, through stories created by the class and Joy. Joy says that these charts "are some of my most meaningful shared reading and writing activities at the beginning of the year."

Every day after the lunch recess, children have thirty minutes of independent reading in reading workshop. Students select their own books from their book bags or from a large collection of leveled books in labeled book baskets. Joy circulates, listening to children read and offering guidance, support, and encouragement.

Joy's students write every day, in their journal and during writing workshop. They write personal narratives, responses to literature, fictional stories, and informational pieces. They write letters and persuasive essays. They write procedures for building a snowman and making a sandwich. Children make excellent use of writing time, and their work is displayed everywhere. Joy's students enjoy writing and sharing their work with others. The skills and independence developed during writing workshop are reflected in their responsible and collaborative behavior during buddy circles. Joy's students see reading and writing as tasks of the world, not simply something they do at school. One child told me how she chose to read during her after-school program, and many talked about reading at home.

Joy's word study program takes many forms. Through shared reading and writing activities she focuses children's attention at the "phonics, word, and sentence level." She plans each lesson based on her ongoing assessment of children's needs through daily observation and frequently administered running records. The children participate in at least one "making words" activity a week and also practice letters and sounds at the ABC center. Joy begins her formal spelling program early in the fall. Children practice five or six words at home each week. These words are "word wall words," or commonly used words students need for their writing. Occasionally, Joy pulls word study games and phonics activities from the reading series teacher's guide to respond to students' needs.

Teachers: Anne Santoro, Cheryl Feeney, Jo-Ann Gettings, and Gia Renaud
Grade Level: Grade 1
Number of Students: Anne, 24; Cheryl and Jo-Ann (team), 21; Gia (inclusion), 17

School Description: Anne Santoro, Jo-Ann Gettings, Cheryl Feeney, and Gia Renaud teach in adjoining first-grade classrooms of a new urban elementary school. Students in all three classrooms come from homes in which English is the first language. School and teachers are in the second year of a grant-funded collaborative literacy initiative supported through a partnership with Lesley University. Grant funding has provided teacher workshops as well as training for Cheryl as a literacy coach. In her capacity as school literacy coordinator, Cheryl moves from class to class supporting implementation of the "literacy collaborative model."

Program Description: All three literacy programs are literature based, and teachers conduct guided reading groups regularly. The school has adopted a reading series that Anne and Gia use as a framework for planning lessons, choosing the stories that best serve students' needs and interests. Because Gia's is an inclusion classroom, she is continually adapting and modifying curriculum for her students. Jo-Ann and Cheryl do not use the series anthology but prefer to teach reading through the use of little books and a variety of instructional reading models.

Grant funding has provided each classroom with a large collection of leveled books for guided reading. There is also a well-stocked "literacy closet" down the hall containing many sets of little books and a library of professional books. Teachers in the building have pooled their collections of books on tape, and these are also housed in the literacy closet for use in classroom listening centers.

Teachers in all three classrooms read aloud to children three or four times a day from picture books in a variety of genres, and children occasionally write reading responses. Shared reading happens in a variety of contexts every day in all rooms. Each classroom has a great many big books, and teachers regularly read and create chart stories and poems with children.

With the help of another building reading specialist, Cheryl and Jo-Ann meet with all children for guided reading every day. Anne meets each of her guided reading groups two or three times a week. Gia conducts more shared reading and individual lessons than her colleagues and meets with guided reading groups only once a week. Students in all three classrooms read with peer partners and independently every day, selecting books from their personal book bags or leveled browsing boxes. Partner reading most often happens first thing in the morning, then again later in the morning as a center activity. In the partner reading center, children are not necessarily paired with a "peer" but may read with stronger or less experienced readers. If not involved with a guided reading group, these teachers circulate during independent and partner reading, conferring and supporting readers.

Students' written work is displayed everywhere in all three classrooms. Chart stories, poems, lists, and classroom reminders line the walls, hang from easels, and are draped on the back of freestanding shelves. In addition to shared reading, all three classrooms do shared and interactive writing daily. "Interactive writing has made a huge difference," says Anne, whose program includes time for daily interactive writing. Children also write in journals, during center time, and during each day's writing workshop. They write during math, science, and social studies, taking notes, recording observations, and writing reflections.

All three classrooms have spelling and word study programs that involve daily practice and extension as well as homework a few nights a week. Anne and Gia use the word study scope and sequence provided by their reading series, adapting and changing it to serve students' needs. Their spelling program "targets a hundred and twenty commonly used words, five of which children practice every week." These words go up on the word wall, are practiced in the ABC and word study centers, and eventually become part of a "no excuse" list children use when revising their writing. Children visit the word study center every day to refine and practice word-solving skills and strategies.

Through their work with the literacy collaborative, Cheryl and Jo-Ann have begun phasing in a new spelling/word study program that emphasizes "principles." Children practice spelling words with partners during daily "buddy spelling." During my visit, they were studying the principle of "r-controlled vowels," reviewing the words on chart paper from the previous day's lesson that illustrated the principle (*car, star, are, far, more,* and *for*).

Teacher: Jenny Baumeister
Grade Level: Grade 1
Number of Students: 20

School Description: Jenny teaches in a large K–5 suburban public school. All students come from homes in which English is the first language.

Program Description: All three first grades at Jenny's school follow a literature-based approach using their district-adopted reading series as a framework while incorporating the following daily routines: teacher read-alouds of fiction and nonfiction; shared reading of charts, poems, big books; guided reading using little books and the stories in their series anthology; independent reading; and buddy reading.

During independent reading and buddy reading, Jenny supports children in choosing just-right books. Hanging on the walls are several charts, listing criteria for just-right books and too-hard books. Jenny tells me that these have been created with the children, and she refers to them frequently at the start of independent or buddy reading.

Jenny and other first-grade teachers use a "work board" to organize center activities. Regular centers include the listening center, writing center, "read the room" center, science center, ABC center, and buddy reading center.

Jenny has a small but growing collection of little books, and her school is just beginning to stock a literacy closet; however, prior to the 2002–03 school year, Jenny had been teaching third grade. Therefore, much of her library is geared toward older readers. Like Christine and Sarah, Jenny needs more books for independent and partner reading. For now, Jenny and her students make the best of the resources they have. Partners make excellent use of the print lining the walls as they read around the room in tandem, revisiting and discussing modeled writing pieces that they have previously composed.

Jenny finds that partner reading is not always productive or collaborative, because a stronger reader will often "take over the reading, deriving all the practice," while the less experienced partner sits silently by. She continues to seek ways to plan and structure partner reading so that children will have opportunity to read with those closest to them in development while also seeking ways to group students flexibly and heterogeneously for other activities.

Teacher: Mary Lee Prescott-Griffin
Grade Level: Grade 1
Number of Students: 15

School Description: I taught in an independent day school with preschool through eighth-grade students. All of my students came from homes in which English was the first language.

Program Description: Mine was a literature-based individualized reading program. Although both first grades followed the school's curriculum scope and sequence and conducted ongoing required assessments (running records, informal reading inventories, miscue analysis, and observations), teachers were free to choose students' reading and writing materials according to the needs of students. Often literature was selected to connect to thematic units of study about animals—birds, mammals, reptiles, and sea creatures.

Every day I read aloud from a chapter book, beginning each year with *Charlotte's Web* (White 1952). I also read three or four picture books throughout the day. Shared reading of charts, poems, and big books usually followed morning circle but might also be incorporated into a minilesson at the start of reading workshop. We sometimes read poems and stories chorally in small groups or as a whole class.

Once a month the entire class read a more challenging "shared book" (they each had their own copy), such as *Ira Sleeps Over* (Waber 1972) or *Henry and Mudge* (Rylant 1994). My teaching partner and I selected shared books for their literary qualities, and over the course of a week or two, we read and reread them many times. Students then took these books home with reminders to parents to keep them handy for practice and rereading. When not reading a "shared book," children selected their own reading books from a large classroom library to read alone or with a partner.

Every day, children read independently, alone or with partners, for at least twenty or thirty minutes. Although I believe individualized reading programs are the most supportive structures for beginning readers, the decision to individualize was made when I had a small class and had enough time to support each reader. When class size grew to twenty or more, I often used guided reading more regularly to ensure that all students received adequate support and scaffolding as they progressed.

Several times each week, children took home WEB books (Wonderfully Exciting Books, an idea borrowed from Regie Routman 2000) that they had practiced at school to read to parents. Students also took home KEEP books (published by The Ohio State Literacy Collaborative) at least once a month during the first half of the year. These inexpensive patterned and predictable books were theirs "to keep," and families received a letter encouraging them to make a special place for the "KEEP library" so that children could return to them again and again for practice.

My first graders read in science, social studies, and math. They also read their own and classmates' "published books," which were typed, bound, and remained in the classroom library until the end of the school year. In conjunction with a yearlong study of animals, children wrote at least four "animal reports," which were also typed and bound in "animal anthologies." Each student received a copy of each anthology to read and take home.

In my program, fluency, decoding, and word analysis were viewed as meaning-making processes, inseparable from comprehension and understanding. I taught skills in context and through direct instruction. During partner reading, children often drew on word-solving strategies to process text together. Throughout the school day, a variety of activities reinforced reading skills and concepts. Daily reading minilessons focused on procedures, process, strategies, and qualities of texts covering a variety of topics. Other activities included "word of the day," phonemic awareness activities, phonics instruction, and a formal spelling program.

I drew from many sources and employed a number of instructional strategies to teach word solving. Most often, word-solving lessons were followed by time for guided and independent practice. Occasionally, I gathered students who needed additional word-solving support into small instructional groups. The first part of the year, I led the class in daily five-minute rhyming games and reproduction activities designed to reinforce children's phonemic awareness. I taught phonics skills as needed and encouraged children to actively apply these skills in context. Several times a week, children worked at ABC and word study centers, practicing and reinforcing letter–sound knowledge and word-solving strategies.

In early November, the children began a formal spelling program, focusing on a small core of words each week. Words might follow familiar sound patterns (e.g., short *a* words) or be taken from commonly used vocabulary lists. Science and social studies vocabulary words were sometimes included as well. Spelling words were practiced through games and activities throughout the week. Once mastered, words became part of students' personal spelling dictionaries kept as reference tools in their writing folders.

On most mornings, writing workshop followed reading, beginning around 11:15. Generally children chose the topics they would write about. At the start of the year, I encouraged them to write from experience. They also wrote letters to pen pals and family members, persuasive pieces, poetry, directions, and informational pieces. Several times a week at the beginning of paired reading or reading workshop, I gave a five-minute book talk, presenting books that children might like to try. These talks represented many genres: fiction, nonfiction, children's own published books, joke books, big books, and poetry.

Bibliography of Children's Books

ALLARD, HARRY, & JAMES MARSHALL. 1977. *Miss Nelson Is Missing.* Boston: Houghton Mifflin.

ALLEY, R. W. 1991. *Old MacDonald Had a Farm.* New York: Grossett & Dunlap.

ARUEGO, JOSE, & ARIANE DEWEY. 1986. *Five Little Ducks.* New York: Crown.

AVI. 1999. *Abigail Takes the Wheel.* New York: HarperCollins.

BENNETT HOPKINS, LEE. 1984. *Surprises.* New York: HarperCollins.

———. 1987. *More Surprises.* New York: HarperCollins.

———. 1992. *Questions: Poems of Wonder.* New York: HarperCollins.

———. 1994. *Weather: Poems for All Seasons.* New York: HarperCollins.

BERENSTAIN, STAN, & JAN BERENSTAIN. 1978. *The Berenstain Bears and the Spooky Old Tree.* New York: Random House.

BERGER, JEANNIE. 2001. *Our Plants.* Boston: Houghton Mifflin.

BLACKSTON, STELLA. 1998. *Bear on a Bike.* New York: Barefoot Books.

BOWES, CLAIRE. 1985. *The Hogboggit.* New York: Richard C. Owen.

BRADDOCK, BETH. 2000. *How Long Do Animals Live?* Huntington Beach, CA: Pacific Learning.

BRIDWELL, NORMAN. 1995. *Clifford and the Big Storm.* New York: Scholastic.

———. Various dates. Various titles. Clifford the Big Red Dog series. New York: Scholastic.

BRONIN, ANDREW. 1975. *Gus and Buster Work Things Out.* New York: Dell.

BROWN, MARC. 1990. *Arthur's Pet Business.* Boston: Little Brown.

———. Various dates. Various titles. Arthur series. Boston: Little Brown.

BUCK, NOLA. 1997. *Oh, Cats!* New York: HarperCollins.

BULLA, CLYDE ROBERT. 1987. *The Chalk Box Kid.* New York: Random House.

CANNARD, ELIZABETH. 1995. *Munching Mark.* Crystal Lake, IL: Rigby.

CARY, ALICE. 1995. *How to Ride a Giraffe.* Boston: Houghton Mifflin.

CHRISTELOW, EILEEN. 1989. *Five Little Monkeys Jumping on the Bed.* New York: Clarion.

COLE, JOANNA. 1986. *Hungry Hungry Sharks.* New York: Random House.

CONRAD, PAM. 1989. *The Tub People.* New York: HarperCollins.

COSTAIN, MEREDITH. 1999. *Animals at Risk.* Littleton, MA: Sundance.

COXE, MOLLY. 1997. *Big Egg.* New York: Random House.

COWLEY, JOY. 1986. *I Can Jump.* Chicago: Wright Group/McGraw-Hill.

———. 1986. *Uncle Buncle's House.* Chicago: Wright Group/McGraw-Hill.

———. 1986. *Up in a Tree.* Chicago: Wright Group/McGraw-Hill.

———. 1987. *Along Comes Jake.* Chicago: Wright Group/McGraw-Hill.

———. 1987. *Monkey Bridge.* Chicago: Wright Group/McGraw-Hill.

———. 1987. *Mr. Grump.* Chicago: Wright Group/McGraw-Hill.

———. 1987. *Noise.* Chicago: Wright Group/McGraw-Hill.

———. 1987. *Ratty Tatty.* Chicago: Wright Group/McGraw-Hill.

———. 1987. *Spider Spider.* Chicago: Wright Group/McGraw-Hill.

———. 1987. *Secret of Spooky House.* Chicago: Wright Group/McGraw-Hill.

———. 1987. *The Tiny Woman's Coat.* Chicago: Wright Group/McGraw-Hill.

———. 1988. *The Biggest Cake in the World.* Katonah, NY: Richard C. Owen.

———. 1989. *Mrs. Wishy-Washy.* Chicago: Wright Group/McGraw-Hill.

———. Various dates. Various titles. Mrs. Wishy-Washy series. Chicago: Wright Group/McGraw-Hill.

DAKOS, KALLI. 1999. *The Bug in the Teacher's Coffee and Other School Poems.* New York: HarperCollins.

GERINGER, LAURA. 1999. *The Stubborn Pumpkin.* New York: Scholastic.

GILES, JENNY. 1997. *Chicken Little.* Crystal Lake, IL: Rigby.

GINSBERG, MIRRA. 1972. *The Chick and the Duckling.* Boston: Houghton Mifflin.

GREENFIELD, ELOISE. 1978. *Honey, I Love and Other Love Poems.* New York: HarperCollins.

———. 1988. *Nathaniel Talking.* New York: Black Butterfly.

HARLEY, BILL. 1996. *Sitting Down to Eat.* Little Rock, AR: August House.

HART, LENNY. 2000. *Seals on the Bus.* New York: Scholastic.

HASTINGS, SCOTT E. 1990. *Miss Mary Mac All Dressed in Black: Tongue Twisters, Jump-Rope Rhymes, and Other Children's Lore from New England.* Little Rock, AR: August House.

HAYWARD, LINDA. 2001. *A Day in the Life of a Police Officer.* New York: DK.

HENKES, KEVIN. 1991. *Chrysanthemum.* New York: Greenwillow.

HILLENBRAND, WILL. 2003. *Here We Go Round the Mulberry Bush.* San Diego, CA: Harcourt.

HOBERMAN, MARY ANN. 2001. *You Read to Me, I'll Read to You: Very Short Stories to Read Together.* Boston: Little Brown.

HOFF, SYD. 1988. *Mrs. Brice's Mice.* New York: HarperCollins.

HOOD, SUSAN. 2000. *Look! I Can Read!* New York: Scholastic.

HUNIA, FRAN. 1977. *Goldilocks and the Three Bears.* Loughborough, UK: Ladybird.

———. 1997. *The Sly Fox and the Red Hen.* Loughborough, UK: Ladybird.

———. 1977. *Three Billy Goats Gruff.* Loughborough, UK: Ladybird.

HUNT, RODERICK, & ALEX BRYCHTA. 1992. *The Secret Room.* New York: Oxford University.

———. 1992. *The Wedding.* New York: Oxford University.

———. 1997. *The Carnival.* New York: Oxford University.

IVERSEN, SANDRA. 2000. *Mother Hippopotamus' Dry Skin.* Chicago: Wright Group/McGraw-Hill.

JAMES, CINDY. 2001. *My Life on an Island.* New York: Rosen.

KATZ, ALAN. 2001. *Take Me Out of the Bathtub and Other Silly Dilly Songs.* New York: Margaret McElderry.

KEATS, EZRA JACK. 1962. *The Snowy Day.* New York: Scholastic.

KRENSKY, STEPHEN. 1999. *Bones.* New York: Random House.

LAURENCE, GLENDA. 1992. *Paul.* Katonah, New York: Richard C. Owen.

LISBERG, RACHEL. 2003. *This Little Light of Mine.* New York: Scholastic.

LOBEL, ARNOLD. 1979. *Days with Frog and Toad.* New York: HarperCollins.

———. Various dates. Various titles. Frog and Toad series. New York: HarperCollins.

MAKAR, BARBARA W. 1980. *Cop Cat.* Cambridge, MA: Educator's Publishing Service.

———. 1980. *The Jet.* Cambridge, MA: Educator's Publishing Service.

———. 1995. *Meg.* Cambridge, MA: Educator's Publishing Service.

MARTIN, BILL, & JOHN ARCHAMBAULT. 1989. *Chicka Chicka Boom Boom.* New York: Simon & Schuster.

MARZOLLO, JEAN. 2003. *I Spy Funny Teeth.* New York: Scholastic.

MAYER, MERCER. 2002. *County Fair.* New York: McGraw-Hill.

———. 2002. *Snow Day.* New York: McGraw-Hill.

McCLOSKEY, SUSAN. 1995. *Look at Me!* Boston: Houghton Mifflin.

MEADOWS, GRAHAM, & CLAIRE VIAL. 2002. *Brown Bears.* New York: Dominie Press.

MEDINA, EDUARDO. 2000. *I Can Draw.* Huntington Beach, CA: Pacific Learning.

MONDO PUBLISHING. 2000. *The Safari Encyclofact.* New York: Author.

MOORE THOMAS, SHELLEY. 2000. *Good Night, Good Knight.* New York: Dutton Children's.

MURPHY, CLAIRE RUDOLF, & JANE G. HAIGH. 2001. *Children of the Gold Rush.* Portland, OR: Alaska Northwest.

NUMEROFF, LAURA JOFFE. 1985. *If You Give a Mouse a Cookie.* New York: Scholastic.

O'CONNOR, JANE. 1986. *The Teeny Tiny Woman.* New York: Random House.

Ohio State University Literacy Collaborative. Various dates. KEEP BOOKS. Columbus: The Ohio State University Literacy Collaborative.

PATERSON, KATHERINE. 2001. *Marvin One Too Many.* New York: HarperCollins.

PETERS, CATHERINE. 1995. *My School.* Wilmington, MA: Great Source Education.

PHINNEY, MARGARET YATSEVITCH. *Will You Play with Me?* New York: Mondo.

PRINCE, SARAH. 1999. *Video Game.* Littleton, MA: Sundance.

RANDELL, BEVERLEY. 1996. *The Pencil.* Crystal Lake, IL: Rigby.

RILEY, KANA. 1995. *Rosie's Pool.* Boston: Houghton Mifflin.

ROBINSON, FAY. 1996. *Great Snakes!* New York: Scholastic.

———. 1999. *Amazing Lizards.* New York: Scholastic.

———. 1999. *Fantastic Frogs.* New York: Scholastic.

ROOP, CONNIE, & PETER ROOP. 2000. *Whales and Dolphins.* New York: Scholastic.

———. 2001. *Octopus Under the Sea.* New York: Scholastic.

ROSIN, MICHAEL & ARTHUR ROBINS. 1990. *Little Rabbit Foo Foo.* New York: Simon & Schuster.

ROTNER, SHELLY & DEN KREISLER. 1996. *Citybook.* In *Hello.* Boston: Houghton Mifflin.

RYLANT, CYNTHIA. 1994. *Henry and Mudge.* Book 1. New York: Scholastic.

———. 1997. *Henry and Mudge Get the Cold Shivers.* New York: Scholastic.

———. 1998. *Henry and Mudge and the Starry Night.* New York: Scholastic.

———. Various dates. Various titles. Cobblestreet Cousins series. New York: Scholastic.

———. Various dates. Various titles. Henry and Mudge series. New York: Scholastic.

SCHAFER, LOLA M. 2000. *We Need Dentists.* Bloomington, MN: Capstone.

SEUSS, DR. 1957. *The Cat in the Hat.* New York: Random House.

STEVENS, BRYNA. 1984. *Deborah Sampson Goes to War.* New York: Dell.

STURGES, PHILEMON. 1999. *The Little Red Hen (Makes a Pizza).* New York: Dutton.

WABER, BERNARD. 1972. *Ira Sleeps Over.* New York: Houghton Mifflin.

WESTCOTT, NADINE B. 1988. *Down by the Bay.* New York: Crown.

———. 1988. *The Lady with the Alligator Purse.* Boston: Little Brown.

———. 1988. *Skip to My Lou.* Boston: Little Brown.

———. 2003. *I Know an Old Lady Who Swallowed a Fly.* Boston: Little Brown.

WHITE, E. B. 1952. *Charlotte's Web.* New York: HarperCollins.

WICKSTROM, SYLVIE KANTOROVITZ. 1985. *Wheels on the Bus.* New York: Crown.

WILLIAMS, ROZANNE LANCZAK. 1994. *Cinderella Dressed in Yellow.* Cypress, CA: Creative Teaching Press.

———. 1994. *I Can Read.* Cypress, CA: Creative Teaching Press.

———. 1994. *I Can Write*. Cypress, CA: Creative Teaching Press.

WINDSOR, JO. 1999. *Scales, Spikes and Armor*. Crystal Lake, IL: Rigby.

WORTH, VALERIE. 1987. *All the Small Poems*. New York: Farrar, Straus.

YOUNG, CHRISTINE. 1993. *The Zoo*. Chicago: Wright Group/McGraw-Hill.

ZIMMERMAN, HEINZ WERNER. 1989. *Henny Penny*. New York: Scholastic.

ZOLOTOW, CHARLOTTE. 2002. *Seasons: A Book of Poems*. New York: HarperCollins.

References

Atwell, Nancie. 1987. *In the Middle: Writing, Reading, and Learning with Adolescents.* Portsmouth, NH: Heinemann Boynton/Cook.

Avery, Carol. 1993. *And with a Light Touch: Learning About Reading, Writing, and Teaching with First Graders.* Portsmouth, NH: Heinemann.

Barnes, Douglas. 1992. *From Communication to Curriculum.* Portsmouth, NH: Heinemann.

Bromley, Karen D'Angelo. 1991. *Webbing with Literature: Creating Story Maps with Children's Books.* Boston: Allyn & Bacon.

Burrill, Nancy, & Nancy Paulson. 1998. *Using Paired Reading to Help Your Students Become Better Readers.* Bellevue, WA: Bureau of Education and Research.

Calkins, Lucy McCormack. 2001. *The Art of Teaching Reading.* New York: Addison Wesley Longman.

Cunningham, Patricia, & Dorothy P. Hall. 1994. *Making Words: Multilevel, Hands-on, Developmentally Appropriate Spelling and Phonics Activities.* Torrance, CA: Good Apple.

Edinger, Monica. 2000. *Seeking History: Teaching with Primary Sources in Grades 4–6.* Portsmouth, NH: Heinemann.

Fosnot, Catherine, ed. 1996. *Constructivism: Theory, Perspectives, and Practice.* New York: Teacher's College Press.

Fountas, Irene C., & Gay Su Pinnell. 1996. *Guided Reading: Good First Teaching for All Children.* Portsmouth, NH: Heinemann.

———. 1999. *Matching Books to Readers: Using Leveled Books in Guided Reading K–3.* Portsmouth, NH: Heinemann.

Griffin, Mary Lee. 2000. "Emergent Readers' Joint Text Construction: A Study of Reading in Social Context." Doctoral dissertation, University of Rhode Island.

———. 2001. "Social Contexts of Beginning Reading." *Language Arts* 78 (4): 371–78.

———. 2002. "Why Don't You Use Your Finger? Paired Reading in First Grade." *The Reading Teacher* 55 (8): 766–74.

Hall, E. T. 1981. *The Silent Language*. New York: Anchor.

Hoyt, Linda. 2000. *Snapshots: Literary Minilessons Up Close*. Portsmouth, NH: Heinemann.

MacGillivray, Laura. 1997. "'I've Seen You Read': Reading Strategies in a First-Grade Class." *Journal of Research in Childhood Education* 11 (2): 135–46.

MacGillivray, Laura, & Shirley Hawes. 1994. "'I Don't Know What I'm Doing—They All Start with *B*': First Graders Negotiate Peer Reading Interactions." *The Reading Teacher* 48 (3): 210–17.

Muldowney, C. J. 1995. "The Effect of a Paired Reading Program on Reading Achievement in a First-Grade Classroom." ERIC, ED379634.

Nes, S. L. 1997. "Less-Skilled Readers: Studying the Effects of Paired Reading on Reading Fluency, Accuracy, Comprehension, Reader Self-Perception, and Lived Experiences." Dissertation Abstracts Online, AAG9736884.

Olby, R. C. 1970. "Francis Crick, DNA, and the Central Dogma." *Daedulus* 99.

Pearson, P. D., & M. C. Gallagher. 1983. "The Instruction of Reading Comprehension." *Contemporary Educational Psychology* 8 (3): 317–44.

Pearson, P. D., & R. J. Tierney. 1984. "On Becoming a Thoughtful Reader: Learning to Read Like a Writer." In *Becoming Readers in a Complex Society,* edited by A. C. Purves & O. Niles, 144–73. 83rd Yearbook of the National Society of the Study of Education. Chicago: The University of Chicago Press.

Prescott-Griffin, Mary Lee, & Nancy L. Witherell. 2004. *Fluency in Focus: Comprehension Strategies for All Young Readers*. Portsmouth, NH: Heinemann.

Rhodes, Lynn K., & Nancy Shanklin. 1993. *Windows into Literacy: Assessing Learners K–8.* Portsmouth, NH: Heinemann.

Routman, Regie. 2000. *Conversations: Strategies for Teaching, Learning, and Evaluating.* Portsmouth, NH: Heinemann.

Samway, Katherine Davies, Gail Whang, & Mary Pippitt. 1995. *Buddy Reading: Cross-Age Tutoring in a Multicultural School.* Portsmouth, NH: Heinemann.

Stone, C. A. 1993. "What Is Missing in the Metaphor of Scaffolding." In *Contexts for Learning: Sociocultural Dynamics in Children's Development,* edited by E. A. Forman, N. Minick, & C. A. Stone. New York: Oxford University Press.

Topping, Keith. 1987. "Paired Reading: A Powerful Technique for Parent Use." *The Reading Teacher* 40: 608–14.

———. 1989. "Peer Tutoring and Paired Reading: Combining Two Powerful Techniques." *The Reading Teacher* 42: 488–94.

Topping, K. J., & G. A. Lindsay.1992. "The Structure and the Development of the Paired Reading Technique." *Journal of Research in Reading* 15 (2): 120–36.

Vygotsky, Lev. 1978. *Mind in Society: The Development of Higher Psychological Processes.* Cambridge: Harvard University Press.

Watson, Dorothy, Carolyn Burke, & Jerome Harste. 1989. *Whole Language: Inquiring Voices.* Richmond Hill, ON: Scholastic-TAB.

Witherell, N. L., & M. C. McMackin. 2002. *Graphic Organizers and Activities for Differentiated Instruction in Reading.* New York: Scholastic.

Wrubel, R. M. 2002. *Great Grouping Strategies: Dozens of Ways to Flexibly Group Your Students for Maximum Learning Across the Curriculum.* New York: Scholastic.

Index

reading interests, 49, 89
reading materials. *See also* books; book selection
    containers for, 27–28
    organizing, 27–30
    refreshing, 29–30
    sending home, 30
    sources of, 12
    supporting collaboration, 89–102
reading partnerships. *See also* partner behavior; peer partnerships
    community building through, 6–8
    friendship and, 74–75, 82, 106, 112
    independence and, 75, 76
    leadership in, 59–60
    naturalness of, 6
    purposes of, 15–16, 82
    roles in, 73
    setting up, 32–36
    for special needs students, 115–17
    student attitudes toward, 74–75
    unbalanced, 60
reading phones, 32
reading pillows, 32
reading responses, 121
reading spaces
    creating, 25–27
    inviting spaces, 27
    personal, 26
    types of, 25–26
"reading the room," 82, 102
reading-writing connection, 21–23
refocusing, student demonstrations of, 65
reluctant readers, book selection for, 48
Renaud, Gia, 113–16, 140–41
repetition of lessons, for English language learners, 119
repetitive choruses, 91
reproducible books, 30
rereading
    for comprehension, 15
    for expression, 121
    favorite books, 49, 78, 101, 117
    for fluency, 15
    value of, 15, 83
retelling stories, 10
    for comprehension, 80
    with puppets, 13–15
    using pictures in, 39
Rhodes, Lynn K., 5
rhyming/rhythmic texts
    for choral reading, 56
    poetry, 96
Rich, Sarah, 9, 10–12, 138
Richardson, Joy, 35, 36, 47, 48, 60, 83–84, 85–86, 140
Roberts, Sharon, xi, 13, 14, 15, 20, 34, 35, 39, 43, 46, 58, 74, 78, 87, 103, 108, 120, 139
Rosie's Pool (Riley), 81, 100
Routman, Regie, 30
Rules for Partners form, 131
Rylant, Cynthia, 49, 99

Safari Encyclofact, The (Mondo Publishing Co.), 99
Samway, Katherine Davies, 4
Santoro, Anne, 24, 35, 40, 47, 81–82, 140–41
scripts, 48
Seals on the Bus (Hart), 95
Seasons: A Book of Poems (Zolotow), 96

seating
    partner positions, 8, 41, 42, 57–58, 107
    seat switching, 8, 105, 113
Secret of Spooky House, The (Cowley), 92
Secret Room, The (Hunt & Brychta), 84
semantic cues, 64
semantic maps, 120
setting, 121
Shanklin, Nancy, 5
shared reading
    for English language learners, 119
    functions of, 18
    modeling fluent reading in, 78
side-by-side seating, 41, 42, 107
Sitting Down to Eat (Harley), 95
skills minilessons, 127
Skip to My Lou (Westcott), 96
Sly Fox and the Red Hen, The (Hunia), 93
Snapshots (Hoyt), 32
social support
    friendship, 74–75, 82, 106, 110, 112
    learning and, xiii
    partner reading and, 5
    for special needs students, 113–14
song-based books, 78, 94–96
special needs students
    inclusion classroom adaptations, 116–17
    peer partnership adaptations for, 113–17
    seat switching and, 113
    social value of partner reading for, 113–14
Spikes, Scales, and Armor (Windsor), 22
standardized testing, 78
story circle form, 135
story maps, 80
strategies
    bookmarks listing, 32, 125–26
    child-centered, xiii
    child-created, 66–73
    for community building, 80–81
    for comprehension building, 79–80, 88
    cueing, 5, 63, 71–73, 108
    discussing, 20, 62
    for emergent readers, 5
    for engagement, 78–81
    for fluency building, 76–79
    hinting, 9–10, 41, 43–44, 110
    for independent reading, 19
    modeling, 12, 103–6
    retelling stories, 10
    sharing, 66–74
    teaching, 39
    text pattern, 5, 119
    tricky-word cards, 11
    word-solving, 11, 13, 19
strategy bookmarks, 32, 125–26
strategy charts, 44–47
    brainstorming ideas for, 44–46
    reviewing, 45–46
    rules for partner reading, 46–47
    for special needs students, 115–16
strategy gloves, 31
structures, for peer reading, 15–16
students
    demonstrations by, 65
    listening to, xi
    organizational behaviors, 73–74